interchange

FIFTH EDITION

T0384681

1A

Student's Book

Jack C. Richards
with Jonathan Hull and Susan Proctor

WITH DIGITAL PACK

CAMBRIDGE
UNIVERSITY PRESS

Shaftesbury Road, Cambridge CB2 8EA, United Kingdom

One Liberty Plaza, 20th Floor, New York, NY 10006, USA

477 Williamstown Road, Port Melbourne, VIC 3207, Australia

314–321, 3rd Floor, Plot 3, Splendor Forum, Jasola District Centre, New Delhi – 110025, India

103 Penang Road, #05-06/07, Visioncrest Commercial, Singapore 238467

Cambridge University Press & Assessment is a department of the University of Cambridge.

We share the University's mission to contribute to society through the pursuit of education, learning and research at the highest international levels of excellence.

www.cambridge.org
Information on this title: www.cambridge.org/9781009040648

First published 2013
Fifth edition 2017
Fifth edition update published 2021

20 19 18 17 16 15 14 13 12 11 10 9 8 7 6

Printed in Poland by Opolgraf

A catalogue record for this publication is available from the British Library

ISBN 978-1-009-04044-0 Student's Book 1 with eBook
ISBN 978-1-009-04047-1 Student's Book 1A with eBook
ISBN 978-1-009-04048-8 Student's Book 1B with eBook
ISBN 978-1-009-04063-1 Student's Book 1 with Digital Pack
ISBN 978-1-009-04064-8 Student's Book 1A with Digital Pack
ISBN 978-1-009-04065-5 Student's Book 1B with Digital Pack
ISBN 978-1-316-62247-6 Workbook 1
ISBN 978-1-316-62254-4 Workbook 1A
ISBN 978-1-316-62266-7 Workbook 1B
ISBN 978-1-108-40606-2 Teacher's Edition 1
ISBN 978-1-316-62226-1 Class Audio 1
ISBN 978-1-009-04066-2 Full Contact with 1 Digital Pack
ISBN 978-1-009-04067-9 Full Contact with 1A Digital Pack
ISBN 978-1-009-04068-6 Full Contact with 1B Digital Pack
ISBN 978-1-108-40305-4 Presentation Plus Level 1

Additional resources for this publication at cambridgeone.org

Informed by teachers

Teachers from all over the world helped develop *Interchange Fifth Edition*. They looked at everything – from the color of the designs to the topics in the conversations – in order to make sure that this course will work in the classroom. We heard from 1,500 teachers in:

- Surveys
- Focus Groups
- In-Depth Reviews

We appreciate the help and input from everyone. In particular, we'd like to give the following people our special thanks:

Jader Franceschi, **Actúa Idiomas,** Bento Gonçalves, Rio Grande do Sul, Brazil

Juliana Dos Santos Voltan Costa, **Actus Idiomas,** São Paulo, Brazil

Ella Osorio, **Angelo State University,** San Angelo, TX, US

Mary Hunter, **Angelo State University,** San Angelo, TX, US

Mario César González, **Angloamericano de Monterrey, SC,** Monterrey, Mexico

Samantha Shipman, **Auburn High School,** Auburn, AL, US

Linda, **Bernick Language School,** Radford, VA, US

Dave Lowrance, **Bethesda University of California,** Yorba Linda, CA, US

Tajbakhsh Hosseini, **Bezmialem Vakif University,** Istanbul, Turkey

Dilek Gercek, **Bil English,** Izmir, Turkey

erkan kolat, **Biruni University, ELT,** Istanbul, Turkey

Nika Gutkowska, **Bluedata International,** New York, NY, US

Daniel Alcocer Gómez, **Cecati 92,** Guadalupe, Nuevo León, Mexico

Samantha Webb, **Central Middle School,** Milton-Freewater, OR, US

Verónica Salgado, **Centro Anglo Americano,** Cuernavaca, Mexico

Ana Rivadeneira Martínez and Georgia P. de Machuca, **Centro de Educación Continua – Universidad Politécnica del Ecuador,** Quito, Ecuador

Anderson Francisco Guimerães Maia, **Centro Cultural Brasil Estados Unidos,** Belém, Brazil

Rosana Mariano, **Centro Paula Souza,** São Paulo, Brazil

Carlos de la Paz Arroyo, Teresa Noemí Parra Alarcón, Gilberto Bastida Gaytan, Manuel Esquivel Román, and Rosa Cepeda Tapia, **Centro Universitario Angloamericano,** Cuernavaca, Morelos, Mexico

Antonio Almeida, **CETEC,** Morelos, Mexico

Cinthia Ferreira, **Cinthia Ferreira Languages Services,** Toronto, ON, Canada

Phil Thomas and Sérgio Sanchez, **CLS Canadian Language School,** São Paulo, Brazil

Celia Concannon, **Cochise College,** Nogales, AZ, US

Maria do Carmo Rocha and CAOP English team, **Colégio Arquidiocesano Ouro Preto – Unidade Cônego Paulo Dilascio,** Ouro Preto, Brazil

Kim Rodriguez, **College of Charleston North,** Charleston, SC, US

Jesús Leza Alvarado, **Coparmex English Institute,** Monterrey, Mexico

John Partain, **Cortazar,** Guanajuato, Mexico

Alexander Palencia Navas, **Cursos de Lenguas, Universidad del Atlántico,** Barranquilla, Colombia

Kenneth Johan Gerardo Steenhuisen Cera, Melfi Osvaldo Guzman Triana, and Carlos Alberto Algarín Jiminez, **Cursos de Lenguas Extranjeras Universidad del Atlantico,** Barranquilla, Colombia

Jane P Kerford, **East Los Angeles College,** Pasadena, CA, US

Daniela, **East Village,** Campinas, São Paulo

Rosalva Camacho Orduño, **Easy English for Groups S.A. de C.V.,** Monterrey, Nuevo León, Mexico

Adonis Gimenez Fusetti, **Easy Way Idiomas,** Ibiúna, Brazil

Eileen Thompson, **Edison Community College,** Piqua, OH, US

Ahminne Handeri O.L Froede, **Englishouse escola de idiomas,** Teófilo Otoni, Brazil

Ana Luz Delgado-Izazola, **Escuela Nacional Preparatoria 5, UNAM,** Mexico City, Mexico

Nancy Alarcón Mendoza, **Facultad de Estudios Superiores Zaragoza, UNAM,** Mexico City, Mexico

Marcilio N. Barros, **Fast English USA,** Campinas, São Paulo, Brazil

Greta Douthat, **FCI Ashland,** Ashland, KY, US

Carlos Lizárraga González, **Grupo Educativo Anglo Americano, S.C.,** Mexico City, Mexico

Hugo Fernando Alcántar Valle, **Instituto Politécnico Nacional, Escuela Superior de Comercio y Administración- Unidad Santotomás, Celex Esca Santo Tomás,** Mexico City, Mexico

Sueli Nascimento, **Instituto Superior de Educação do Rio de Janeiro,** Rio de Janeiro, Brazil

Elsa F Monteverde, **International Academic Services,** Miami, FL, US

Laura Anand, **Irvine Adult School,** Irvine, CA, US

Prof. Marli T. Fernandes (principal) and Prof. Dr. Jefferson J. Fernandes (pedagogue), **Jefferson Idiomass,** São Paulo, Brazil

Herman Bartelen, **Kanda Gaigo Gakuin,** Tokyo, Japan

Cassia Silva, **Key Languages,** Key Biscayne, FL, US

Sister Mary Hope, **Kyoto Notre Dame Joshi Gakuin,** Kyoto, Japan

Nate Freedman, **LAL Language Centres,** Boston, MA, US

Richard Janzen, **Langley Secondary School,** Abbotsford, BC, Canada

Christina Abel Gabardo, **Language House,** Campo Largo, Brazil

Ivonne Castro, **Learn English International,** Cali, Colombia

Julio Cesar Maciel Rodrigues, **Liberty Centro de Línguas,** São Paulo, Brazil

Ann Gibson, **Maynard High School,** Maynard, MA, US

Martin Darling, **Meiji Gakuin Daigaku,** Tokyo, Japan

Dax Thomas, **Meiji Gakuin Daigaku,** Yokohama, Kanagawa, Japan

Derya Budak, **Mevlana University,** Konya, Turkey

B Sullivan, **Miami Valley Career Technical Center International Program,** Dayton, OH, US

Julio Velazquez, **Milo Language Center,** Weston, FL, US

Daiane Siqueira da Silva, Luiz Carlos Buontempo, Marlete Avelina de Oliveira Cunha, Marcos Paulo Segatti, Morgana Eveline de Oliveira, Nadia Lia Gino Alo, and Paul Hyde Budgen, **New Interchange-Escola de Idiomas,** São Paulo, Brazil

Patrícia França Furtado da Costa, Juiz de Fora, Brazil
Patricia Servín

Chris Pollard, **North West Regional College SK,** North Battleford, SK, Canada

Olga Amy, **Notre Dame High School,** Red Deer, Canada

Amy Garrett, **Ouachita Baptist University,** Arkadelphia, AR, US

Mervin Curry, **Palm Beach State College,** Boca Raton, FL, US

Julie Barros, **Quality English Studio,** Guarulhos, São Paulo, Brazil

Teodoro González Saldaña and Jesús Monserrrta Mata Franco, **Race Idiomas,** Mexico City, Mexico

Autumn Westphal and Noga La`or, **Rennert International,** New York, NY, US

Antonio Gallo and Javy Palau, **Rigby Idiomas,** Monterrey, Mexico Tatiane Gabriela Sperb do Nascimento, **Right Way,** Igrejinha, Brazil

Mustafa Akgül, **Selahaddin Eyyubi Universitesi,** Diyarbakır, Turkey

James Drury M. Fonseca, **Senac Idiomas Fortaleza,** Fortaleza, Ceara, Brazil

Manoel Fialho S Neto, **Senac – PE,** Recife, Brazil

Jane Imber, **Small World,** Lawrence, KS, US

Tony Torres, **South Texas College,** McAllen, TX, US

Janet Rose, **Tennessee Foreign Language Institute,** College Grove, TN, US

Todd Enslen, **Tohoku University,** Sendai, Miyagi, Japan

Daniel Murray, **Torrance Adult School,** Torrance, CA, US

Juan Manuel Pulido Mendoza, **Universidad del Atlántico,** Barranquilla, Colombia

Juan Carlos Vargas Millán, **Universidad Libre Seccional Cali,** Cali (Valle del Cauca), Colombia

Carmen Cecilia Llanos Ospina, **Universidad Libre Seccional Cali,** Cali, Colombia

Jorge Noriega Zenteno, **Universidad Politécnica del Valle de México,** Estado de México, Mexico

Aimee Natasha Holguin S., **Universidad Politécnica del Valle de México UPVM,** Tultitlàn Estado de México, Mexico

Christian Selene Bernal Barraza, **UPVM Universidad Politécnica del Valle de México,** Ecatepec, Mexico

Lizeth Ramos Acosta, **Universidad Santiago de Cali,** Cali, Colombia

Silvana Dushku, **University of Illinois Champaign,** IL, US

Deirdre McMurtry, **University of Nebraska – Omaha,** Omaha, NE, US

Jason E Mower, **University of Utah,** Salt Lake City, UT, US

Paul Chugg, **Vanguard Taylor Language Institute,** Edmonton, Alberta, Canada

Henry Mulak, **Varsity Tutors,** Los Angeles, CA, US

Shirlei Strucker Calgaro and Hugo Guilherme Karrer, **VIP Centro de Idiomas,** Panambi, Rio Grande do Sul, Brazil

Eleanor Kelly, **Waseda Daigaku Extension Centre,** Tokyo, Japan

Sherry Ashworth, **Wichita State University,** Wichita, KS, US

Laine Bourdene, **William Carey University,** Hattiesburg, MS, US

Serap Aydın, Istanbul, Turkey

Liliana Covino, Guarulhos, Brazil

Yannuarys Jiménez, Barranquilla, Colombia

Juliana Morais Pazzini, Toronto, ON, Canada

Marlon Sanches, Montreal, Canada

Additional content contributed by Kenna Bourke, Inara Couto, Nic Harris, Greg Manin, Ashleigh Martinez, Laura McKenzie, Paul McIntyre, Clara Prado, Lynne Robertson, Mari Vargo, Theo Walker, and Maria Lucia Zaorob.

Plan of Book 1A

Titles/Topics	Speaking	Grammar
UNIT 1 PAGES 2–7		
Where are you from? Introductions and greetings; names, countries, and nationalities	Introducing oneself; introducing someone; checking information; exchanging personal information; saying hello and good-bye; talking about school subjects	Wh-questions and statements with *be*; questions with *what*, *where*, *who*, and *how*; yes/no questions and short answers with *be*; subject pronouns; possessive adjectives
UNIT 2 PAGES 8–13		
What do you do? Jobs, workplaces, and school; daily schedules; clock time	Describing work and school; asking for and giving opinions; describing daily schedules	Simple present Wh-questions and statements; question: *when*; time expressions: *at, in, on, around, early, late, until, before,* and *after*
PROGRESS CHECK PAGES 14–15		
UNIT 3 PAGES 16–21		
How much are these? Shopping and prices; clothing and personal items; colors and materials	Talking about prices; giving opinions; discussing preferences; making comparisons; buying and selling things	Demonstratives: *this, that, these, those; one* and *ones;* questions: *how much* and *which;* comparisons with adjectives
UNIT 4 PAGES 22–27		
Do you play the guitar? Music, movies, and TV shows; entertainers; invitations and excuses; dates and times	Talking about likes and dislikes; giving opinions; making invitations and excuses	Yes/no and Wh-questions with *do;* question: *what kind;* object pronouns; modal verb *would;* verb + *to* + verb
PROGRESS CHECK PAGES 28–29		
UNIT 5 PAGES 30–35		
What an interesting family! Family members; typical families	Talking about families and family members; exchanging information about the present; describing family life	Present continuous yes/no and Wh-questions, statements, and short answers; quantifiers: *all, nearly all, most, many, a lot of, some, not many,* and *few;* pronoun: *no one*
UNIT 6 PAGES 36–41		
How often do you run? Sports, fitness activities, and exercise; routines	Asking about and describing routines and exercise; talking about frequency; discussing sports and athletes; talking about abilities	Adverbs of frequency: *always, almost always, usually, often, sometimes, hardly ever, almost never,* and *never;* questions: *how often, how long, how well,* and *how good;* short answers
PROGRESS CHECK PAGES 42–43		
UNIT 7 PAGES 44–49		
We went dancing! Free-time and weekend activities	Talking about past events; giving opinions about past experiences; talking about vacations	Simple past yes/no and Wh-questions, statements, and short answers with regular and irregular verbs; past of *be*
UNIT 8 PAGES 50–55		
How's the neighborhood? Stores and places in a city; neighborhoods; houses and apartments	Asking about and describing locations of places; asking about and describing neighborhoods; asking about quantities	*There is/there are; one, any,* and *some;* prepositions of place; quantifiers; questions: *how many* and *how much;* count and noncount nouns
PROGRESS CHECK PAGES 56–57		
GRAMMAR PLUS PAGES 132–149		

Where are you from?

▶ Introduce oneself and others
▶ Talk about oneself and learn about others

1 CONVERSATION Please call me Alexa.

▶ Listen and practice.

Arturo: Hello, I'm Arturo Valdez.

Alexa: Hi. My name is Alexandra Costa, but please call me Alexa.

Arturo: OK. Where are you from, Alexa?

Alexa: Brazil. How about you?

Arturo: I'm from Mexico.

Alexa: Oh, I love Mexico! It's really beautiful. Oh, good. Soo-jin is here.

Arturo: Who's Soo-jin?

Alexa: She's my classmate. We're in the same business class.

Arturo: Where's she from?

Alexa: South Korea. Let's go and say hello. Sorry, what's your last name again? Vargas?

Arturo: Actually, it's Valdez.

Alexa: How do you spell that?

Arturo: V-A-L-D-E-Z.

2 SPEAKING Checking information

A PAIR WORK Introduce yourself with your full name. Use the expressions in the box. Talk to the classmate sitting next to you and to three more classmates.

A: Hi! I'm Akemi Shimizu.

B: I'm sorry. What's your last name again?

A: Shimizu.

B: How do you spell that?

B CLASS ACTIVITY Tell the class the name of the first classmate you talked to. Make a list of names.

"Her name is Akemi Shimizu. She spells her name . . ."

useful expressions
Hi! I'm . . .
I'm sorry. What's your first / last name again?
How do you spell that?
What do people call you?

3 CONVERSATION This is Arturo Valdez.

▶ **A** Listen and practice.

Alexa: Hi Soo-jin, this is Arturo Valdez. He's a biology student.

Soo-jin: Nice to meet you, Arturo. I'm Soo-jin Kim.

Arturo: Hi. So, you're from South Korea?

Soo-jin: That's right. I'm from Seoul.

Arturo: Cool! What's Seoul like?

Soo-jin: It's really nice. It's a very exciting city.

▶ **B** Listen to the rest of the conversation. What city is Arturo from? What's it like?

4 PRONUNCIATION Linked sounds

▶ Listen and practice. Notice how final consonant sounds are often linked to the vowels that follow them.

I'm a biology student.   My friend is over there.   My name is Alexandra Costa.

5 GRAMMAR FOCUS

▶ **Statements with *be*; possessive adjectives**

Statements with *be*	Contractions of *be*	Possessive adjectives
I**'m** from Mexico.	I**'m** = I am	my
You**'re** from Brazil.	you**'re** = you are	your
He**'s** from Japan.	he**'s** = he is	his
She**'s** a business student.	she**'s** = she is	her
It**'s** an exciting city.	it**'s** = it is	its
We**'re** in the same class.	we**'re** = we are	our
They**'re** my classmates.	they**'re** = they are	their

GRAMMAR PLUS *see page 132*

A Complete these sentences. Then tell a partner about yourself.

1. _____My_____ name is Aiko Yoshida. _____ from Japan. _____ family is in Nagoya. _____ brother is a college student. _____ name is Haruki.

2. _____ name is Matias. _____ from Santiago. _____ a really nice city. _____ sister is a student here. _____ parents are in Chile right now.

3. _____ Angelica, but everyone calls me Angie. _____ last name is Newton. _____ a student at City College. _____ parents are on vacation this week. _____ in Las Vegas.

▶ **Wh-questions with be**

Where's your friend?	He's in class.
Who's Soo-jin?	She's my classmate.
What's Seoul **like**?	It's a very exciting city.
Where are you and Vanessa from?	We're from Brazil.
How are your classes?	They're pretty interesting.
What are your classmates **like**?	They're really nice.

GRAMMAR PLUS *see page 132*

For a list of countries and nationalities, see the appendix at the back of the book.

B Complete these questions. Then practice with a partner.

1. **A:** _____Who's_____ that?
   B: Oh, that's Mrs. Adams.
2. **A:** _____ she from?
   B: She's from San Diego.
3. **A:** _____ her first name?
   B: It's Caroline.

4. **A:** _____ the two students over there?
   B: Their names are Mason and Ava.
5. **A:** _____ they from?
   B: They're from Vancouver.
6. **A:** _____ they _____?
   B: They're shy, but very friendly.

C **GROUP WORK** Write five questions about your classmates.
Then ask and answer the questions.

> What's your last name?
>
> Where's Jay from?

6 SNAPSHOT

SCHOOL SUBJECTS

1 _____math_____

2 _____

3 _____

4 _____

5 _____

6 _____

7 _____

8 _____

Write the names of the school subjects under the pictures.
What is (or was) your favorite school subject?
What subjects don't (or didn't) you like?

math	literature
history	chemistry
physics	geography
biology	physical education

7 CONVERSATION How's it going?

▶ Listen and practice.

Arturo Hi, Soo-jin!

Soo-jin Hey Arturo. How's it going?

Arturo Great! How are you?

Soo-jin I'm fine, thanks. So, are your classes interesting this semester?

Arturo Yes, they are. I really love biology.

Soo-jin Biology? Are you and Alexa in the same class?

Arturo No, we aren't. My class is in the morning. Her class is in the afternoon.

Soo-jin Oh, OK. Hey, do you have time for coffee?

Arturo Sure. I'd love some coffee.

8 GRAMMAR FOCUS

▶ **Yes/No questions and short answers with** *be*

Are you free?	Yes, I **am**.	No, I**'m not**.
Is Arturo from Mexico?	Yes, he **is**.	No, he**'s not**./No, he **isn't**.
Is Alexa's class in the morning?	Yes, it **is**.	No, it**'s not**./No, it **isn't**.
Are you and Alexa in the same class?	Yes, we **are**.	No, we**'re not**./No, we **aren't**.
Are your classes interesting?	Yes, they **are**.	No, they**'re not**./No, they **aren't**.

GRAMMAR PLUS *see page 132*

A Complete the conversations. Then practice with a partner.

1. **A:** ____Is____ Mr. Jones from the United States?
   B: Yes, he _____. _____ from Baltimore.

2. **A:** _____ English class at 2:00?
   B: No, it _____. _____ at 3:00.

3. **A:** _____ you and Giovanna from Italy?
   B: Yes, we _____. _____ from Milan.

4. **A:** _____ Mr. and Mrs. Flores Brazilian?
   B: No, they _____. _____ Peruvian.

B Answer these questions. If you answer "no," give the correct information. Then ask your partner the questions.

1. Are you from the United States? _____
2. Is your teacher from Canada? _____
3. Is your English class in the morning? _____
4. Are you free after class? _____

C GROUP WORK Write five questions about your classmates. Then ask and answer the questions.

Are Kate and Phil from Chicago?

9 WORD POWER Hello and good-bye

A Do you know these expressions? Which ones are "hellos" and which ones are "good-byes"? Complete the chart. Add expressions of your own.

✓ Bye.
✓ Good morning.
Good night.
Have a good day.
Hey.
Hi.

How are you?
How's it going?
See you later.
See you tomorrow.
Talk to you later.
What's up?

Hello	Good-bye
Good morning.	Bye.

B Match each expression with the best response.

1. Have a good day.
2. Hi. How are you?
3. What's up?
4. Good morning.

a. Oh, not much.
b. Thank you. You, too.
c. Good morning.
d. Pretty good, thanks.

C **CLASS ACTIVITY** Practice saying hello. Then practice saying good-bye.

A: Hi, Sakura. How's it going?
B: Pretty good, thanks. How are you?

10 LISTENING Everyone calls me Bill.

▶ Listen to the conversations. Complete the information about each person.

First name	Last name	Where from?	What do they study?
1. William			
2.	Ortiz		
3. Min-soo			

11 INTERCHANGE 1 Getting to know you

Find out about your classmates. Go to Interchange 1 on page 114.

A Look at the names in the article. Are any of the names popular in your country? What similar names can you think of?

IS YOUR NAME *Trendy?*

Some people have names that are very unusual and unique. Think about the actress Emily Blunt, for example. Her daughters' names are Hazel (an eye color) and Violet (a flower). Alicia Keys has a son named Egypt. How cool is that? Are these names trendy? The answer is . . . maybe.

Many names seem to be trendy for a while, just like clothes. In the United States, some grandmothers and great-grandmothers have names like Mildred and Dorothy. For grandfathers and great-grandfathers, it's old names like Eugene or Larry. These names usually come from Greek and Latin, but they're not very popular now.

Parents sometimes choose names because they like an actor or a famous person. That's how trends usually start. For example, David and Victoria Beckham have a son named Brooklyn and a daughter named Harper. Now, Brooklyn is a popular boy's name and Harper is a popular girl's name. In the United Kingdom, baby boys often get the name George because of Prince George, Prince William and Kate Middleton's first child.

There is also a trend for names that are things or places (like Egypt). Flower names are becoming more popular: Poppy, Daisy, and Lotus, for example. Space names are cool, too. More and more babies have names like Orion (a star), Luna (the moon), or Mars (a planet).

POPULAR NAMES FOR BOYS & GIRLS

Can you guess who helped make these names popular?

BOYS	GIRLS
Bruno	January
Leonardo	Angelina
Liam	Audrey

Bruno Mars, Leonardo di Caprio, Liam Hemsworth, January Jones, Angelina Jolie, Audrey Hepburn

B Read the article. Then check (✓) the sentences that are true.

- [ ] **1.** Baby names like Mildred and Larry aren't so trendy now.
- [ ] **2.** Many babies are named after clothes.
- [ ] **3.** Alicia Keys has a son named Hazel.
- [ ] **4.** There is a famous prince named George.
- [ ] **5.** Some girls' names are the same as flower names.
- [ ] **6.** Babies never have names that are the same as planets or stars.

C **GROUP WORK** What names do you like? Can you think of anyone with an unusual name? Do you know how they got that name? Tell your classmates.

2 What do you do?

▸ Ask and answer questions about jobs
▸ Describe routines and daily schedules

1 SNAPSHOT

Six Popular Part-time Jobs in the United States

babysitter

fitness instructor

office assistant

sales associate

social media assistant

tutor

Which jobs are easy? difficult? exciting? boring? Why?
Are these good jobs for students? What are some other part-time jobs?

2 WORD POWER Jobs

A Complete the word map with jobs from the list.

✓ accountant
✓ cashier
  chef
✓ dancer
✓ flight attendant
  musician
  pilot
  receptionist
  server
  singer
  tour guide
  web designer

OFFICE WORK
accountant
_____
_____
_____
_____

FOOD SERVICE
cashier
_____
_____
_____
_____

JOBS

TRAVEL INDUSTRY
flight attendant
_____
_____
_____
_____

ENTERTAINMENT BUSINESS
dancer
_____
_____
_____
_____

B Add two more jobs to each category. Then compare with a partner.

3 SPEAKING Work and workplaces

GROUP WORK Form teams. One team member sits with his or her back to the board. Choose a job from page 8 or from the box. Write the job on the board. Your team member asks yes/no questions and tries to guess the job.

More jobs	
carpenter	nurse
cook	office manager
dentist	police officer
doctor	reporter
engineer	restaurant host
firefighter	salesperson
front desk clerk	security guard
graphic designer	taxi driver
lawyer	teacher
mechanic	vendor

A: Does the person work in a hospital?
B: No, he or she doesn't.

A: Does he or she work in a restaurant?
C: Yes, that's right!

4 CONVERSATION I'm on my feet all day.

▶ **A** Listen and practice.

Amy What do you do, Derek?

Derek I work part-time as a server.

Amy Oh, really? What restaurant do you work at?

Derek I work at Stella's Café downtown.

Amy That's cool. How do you like it?

Derek It's OK. I'm on my feet all day, so I'm always tired. What do you do?

Amy I'm a dancer.

Derek A dancer! How exciting!

Amy Yeah, it's great! I work with incredible people.

Derek That sounds really nice. But is it difficult?

Amy A little. I'm on my feet all day, too, but I love it.

▶ **B** Listen to the rest of the conversation. Who does Amy travel with? Who does she meet in other cities?

▶ **Simple present Wh-questions and statements**

What do you **do**?	I'**m** a student. I **have** a part-time job, too.	
Where do you **work**?	I **work** at a restaurant.	
Where do you **go** to school?	I **go** to the University of Texas.	
What does Amy **do**?	She'**s** a dancer.	
Where does she **work**?	She **works** at a dance company.	
	She **travels**, too.	
How does she **like** it?	She **loves** it.	

I/You	He/She
work	works
take	takes
study	studies
teach	teaches
do	does
go	goes
have	has

GRAMMAR PLUS *see page 133*

A Complete these conversations. Then practice with a partner.

1. A: What _____*do*_____ you _____*do*_____?
  B: I'm a full-time student. I study the piano.
  A: And _____ do you _____ to school?
  B: I _____ to the Brooklyn School of Music.
  A: Wow! _____ do you like your classes?
  B: I _____ them a lot.

2. A: What _____ Tanya do?
  B: She's a teacher. She _____ an art class at a school in Denver.
  A: And what about Ryan? Where _____ he work?
  B: He _____ for a big computer company in San Francisco.
  A: _____ does he do, exactly?
  B: He's a web designer. He _____ fantastic websites.

3. A: What _____ Bruce and Ivy do?
  B: They _____ at an Italian restaurant. It's really good.
  A: That's nice. _____ is Ivy's job?
  B: Well, she manages the finances and Bruce _____ in the kitchen.

4. A: Where _____ Ali work?
  B: He _____ at the university. He _____ a part-time job.
  A: Really? What _____ he do?
  B: He _____ office work.
  A: How _____ he like it?
  B: Not much, but he _____ some extra money to spend!

B **PAIR WORK** Ask your partner questions like these about work and school. Take notes to use in Exercise 6.

What do you do?
Do you go to school or do you have a job?
How do you like . . . ?
Do you study another language?
What's your favorite . . . ?
What does your best friend do?

C **CLASS WORK** Tell the class about your partner.

"Regina goes to Chicago University, and she has a part-time job, too. She likes . . ."

6 WRITING A biography

A Use your notes from Exercise 5 to write a biography of your partner. Don't use your partner's name. Use *he* or *she* instead.

> My partner is a chef. She works in a very nice restaurant near our school. She cooks Italian food and bakes desserts. She likes her English classes a lot. Her favorite activities are speaking and vocabulary practice. She studies another language, too . . .

B CLASS ACTIVITY Pass your biographies around the class. Guess who each biography is about.

7 CONVERSATION I work in the afternoon.

A Listen and practice.

	KRISTINA	I need to go to National Bank downtown, please. I'm late for a meeting.
	TAXI DRIVER	No problem. What time is your meeting?
	KRISTINA	In 10 minutes! I don't usually work in the morning.
	TAXI DRIVER	Really? What time do you usually go to work?
	KRISTINA	I work in the afternoon. I start at one.
	TAXI DRIVER	That's pretty late. Do you like to work in the afternoon?
	KRISTINA	Yes, I do. I work better in the afternoon. I finish at seven or eight, then I go home and eat dinner at around 10:30.
	TAXI DRIVER	Wow, you have dinner late! I go to bed every night at 8:00.
	KRISTINA	Really? That seems so early!

B Listen to the rest of the conversation. What time does the taxi driver start work? What time does he finish?

8 PRONUNCIATION Syllable stress

A Listen and practice. Notice which syllable has the main stress.

● ● ●
dancer

● ● ●
salesperson

● ● ●
accountant

_____ _____ _____

_____ _____ _____

B Which stress pattern do these words have? Add them to the columns in part A. Then listen and check.

carpenter   musician   firefighter   reporter   server   tutor

▶ Time expressions

I get up	**at** 7:00	**in** the morning	**on** weekdays.	Expressing clock time
I leave work	**early**	**in** the afternoon	**on** Thursdays.	7:00
I go to bed	**around** eleven	**in** the evening	**on** weeknights.	seven
I get home	**late**	**at** night	**on** weekends.	seven o'clock
I stay up	**until** midnight	**on** Fridays.		7:00 A.M. = 7:00 in the morning
I exercise	**before** noon	**on** Saturdays.		7:00 P.M. = 7:00 in the evening
I wake up	**after** noon	**on** Sundays.		

GRAMMAR PLUS *see page 133*

A Choose the correct word.

1. I get up (at)/ **until** six **at** / **on** weekdays.
2. I have lunch **at** / **early** 11:30 **in** / **on** Mondays.
3. I have a snack **in** / **around** 10:00 **in** / **at** night.
4. **In** / **On** Fridays, I leave school **early** / **before**.
5. I stay up **before** / **until** 1:00 A.M. **in** / **on** weekends.
6. I sleep **around** / **until** noon **in** / **on** Sundays.

7. I have dinner **at** / **in** 7:00 **at** / **on** weeknights.
8. I read a book **after** / **before** I go to sleep.
9. **In** / **On** weekends, I go to bed **in** / **at** 1:00 A.M.
10. **In** / **On** Thursdays, I leave work **at** / **in** 9:00 P.M.
11. I work **late** / **until** on Wednesdays.
12. I study **around** / **until** 11:00 **after** / **early** dinner.

B Rewrite the sentences in part A so that they are true for you. Then compare with a partner.

C **PAIR WORK** Take turns asking and answering these questions.

1. Which days do you get up early? late?
2. What's something you do in the morning?
3. What's something you do before English class?
4. What's something you do on Saturday evenings?
5. Which days do you stay up late?
6. Which days do you go to bed early?
7. What do you do after dinner on weeknights?
8. What do you do after lunch on weekends?

10 LISTENING What hours do you work?

▶ A Listen to Aaron, Madison, and Kayla talk about their daily schedules. Complete the chart.

	Aaron	Madison	Kayla
Job	carpenter		
Gets up at . . .		7:00 a.m.	
Gets home at . . .			
Goes to bed at . . .			

B **CLASS ACTIVITY** Who do you think has the best daily schedule? Why?

11 INTERCHANGE 2 What we have in common

Find out about your classmates' schedules. Go to Interchange 2 on page 115.

A Read the title and skim the blog posts. What are these people's jobs? Why do you think their jobs are hard to understand?

MY PARENTS DON'T UNDERSTAND MY JOB!

DANNY BANGKOK, THAILAND

Do you know what a social media manager is? Right, of course you do, but my mom doesn't. Every week, I try to explain my job to her. I work for a company that makes cars. My job is to tell the world how great our cars are. How do I do that? I get up early and write posts for social media. On weekdays, I go online around 7:00 a.m. and sometimes I work until 9:00 at night. The problem is . . . my mom doesn't use social media.

CARLA BUENOS AIRES, ARGENTINA

It's so funny! I explain my job to my dad, but he just looks very confused. I'm a fashion designer. I always get up early on weekdays because I love my job. I have an office, and most days I draw pictures of cool new clothes, like dresses, jeans, and T-shirts. I also go to stores to look at fabrics to use for my clothes. My dad thinks I'm crazy! He just goes to a store and buys stuff to wear. He doesn't know someone has to design it first.

NICO ATHENS, GREECE

So, I'm a sociologist. I study people. Well, I study how people behave. I also study why they behave the way they do. My mom and dad don't understand why I do that. My mom says, "Nico, people are people! They just do normal things!" I don't agree. There are many reasons why people do the things they do, and I love to learn about that.

LISA LOS ANGELES, UNITED STATES

I'm a software engineer, but my dad doesn't know what that means. I tell him that software is the technology inside his computer, his phone, and his tablet. I make apps for smartphones. One app helps people exercise more. It's very cool because it tracks everything you do during the day. You put your phone in your pocket, and the app does the rest. The app tracks your walk to school, your bike ride on the weekend, and more.

B Read the article. Who does the following things? Check (✓) the correct boxes.

Who does something . . .	Danny	Carla	Nico	Lisa
1. . . . to help people get fit?	☐	☐	☐	☐
2. . . . to understand other people?	☐	☐	☐	☐
3. . . . to make things you can wear?	☐	☐	☐	☐
4. . . . to tell other people about their company?	☐	☐	☐	☐

C PAIR WORK Which of the four jobs do you think is the most interesting? the most useful? the hardest to explain? What other things are hard to explain? Think about different jobs, hobbies, or classes at school.

Units 1–2 Progress check

SELF-ASSESSMENT

How well can you do these things? Check (✔) the boxes.

I can . . .	Very well	OK	A little
Make an introduction and use basic greeting expressions (Ex. 1)	☐	☐	☐
Show I didn't understand and ask for repetition (Ex. 1)	☐	☐	☐
Ask and answer questions about myself and other people (Ex. 2)	☐	☐	☐
Ask and answer questions about work (Ex. 3, 4)	☐	☐	☐
Ask and answer questions about habits and routines (Ex. 5)	☐	☐	☐

1 ROLE PLAY Introductions

A PAIR WORK You are talking to someone at school. Have a conversation.
Then change roles and try the role play again.

A: Hi. How are you?
B: . . .
A: By the way, my name is . . .
B: I'm sorry. What's your name again?
A: . . .
B: I'm . . . . Are you a student here?
A: . . . And how about you?
B: . . .
A: Oh, really? And where are you from?

B GROUP WORK Join another pair.
Introduce your partner.

2 SPEAKING Interview

Write questions for these answers. Then use the questions to interview a classmate.

1.  What's _____ ?   My name is Midori Oki.
2. _____ ?   I'm from Kyoto, Japan.
3. _____ ?   Yes, my classes are very interesting.
4. _____ ?   My favorite class is English.
5. _____ ?   No, my teacher isn't American.
6. _____ ?   My classmates are very nice.
7. _____ ?   My best friend is Kiara.

3 SPEAKING What a great job!

A What do you know about these jobs? List three things each person does.

software engineer

caregiver

electrician

IT worker

works on a computer _____ _____ _____

_____ _____ _____ _____

B GROUP WORK Compare your lists. Take turns asking about the jobs.

4 LISTENING At Dylan's party

▶ A Listen to Austin and Haley talk about work and school. Complete the chart.

	Austin	Haley
What do you do?		
Where do you work/study?		
How do you like your job/classes?		
What do you do after work/school?		

B PAIR WORK Practice the questions in part A. Answer with your own information.

5 SPEAKING Survey: My perfect day

A Imagine your perfect day. Read the questions, then add one more.
Then write your answers.

What time do you get up? _____

What do you do after you get up? _____

Where do you go? _____

What do you do in the evening? _____

When do you go to bed? _____

_____

B PAIR WORK Talk about your perfect day. Answer any questions.

WHAT'S NEXT?

Look at your Self-assessment again. Do you need to review anything?

How much are these?

▸ **Ask about and describe prices**
▸ **Discuss preferences**

1 SNAPSHOT

WHAT'S IN A **COLOR?**

white = hopeful
blue = truthful
brown = friendly
black = powerful

green = jealous
yellow = happy
orange = confident
red = exciting
pink = loving
purple = creative
gray = sad

Which words have a positive meaning? Which have a negative meaning?
What meanings do these colors have for you? What colors do you like to wear?

2 CONVERSATION I'll take it!

▸ **A** Listen and practice.

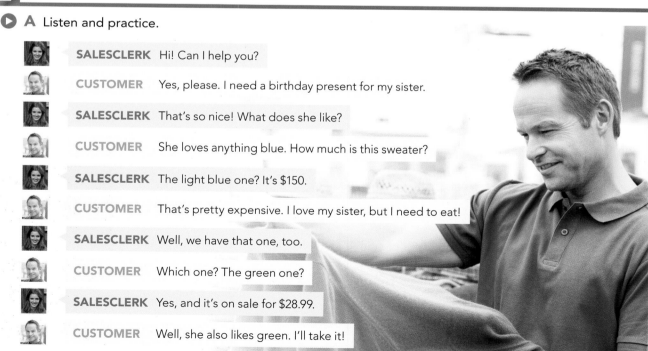

SALESCLERK Hi! Can I help you?

CUSTOMER Yes, please. I need a birthday present for my sister.

SALESCLERK That's so nice! What does she like?

CUSTOMER She loves anything blue. How much is this sweater?

SALESCLERK The light blue one? It's $150.

CUSTOMER That's pretty expensive. I love my sister, but I need to eat!

SALESCLERK Well, we have that one, too.

CUSTOMER Which one? The green one?

SALESCLERK Yes, and it's on sale for $28.99.

CUSTOMER Well, she also likes green. I'll take it!

▸ **B** Listen to the rest of the conversation. What else does the customer look at? Does he buy it?

3 GRAMMAR FOCUS

▶ Demonstratives; one, ones

▶ **saying prices**

99¢ = ninety-nine cents

$28 = twenty-eight dollars

$28.99 = twenty-eight ninety-nine

How much is	**this** T-shirt?	**that** T-shirt?	Which **one**?	
	this one?	**that one**?	The blue **one**.	**It's** $28.99.
How much are	**these** sneakers?	**those** sneakers	Which **ones**?	
	these?	**those**?	The gray **ones**.	**They're** $40.

GRAMMAR PLUS *see page 134*

A Complete these conversations. Then practice with a partner.

A: Excuse me. How much are

_____*those*_____ jeans?

B: Which _____? Do you mean

_____?

A: No, the light blue _____.

B: Oh, _____ are $59.95.

A: Wow! That's expensive!

A: How much is _____ backpack?

B: Which _____?

A: The orange _____.

B: It's $36.99. But _____ green

_____ is only $22.25.

A: That's not bad. Can I see it, please?

B **PAIR WORK** Add prices to the items. Then ask and answer questions.

A: How much are these boots?

B: Which ones?

A: The brown ones.

B: They're $95.50.

A: That's expensive!

useful expressions

That's cheap.

That's reasonable.

That's OK/not bad.

That's expensive.

4 PRONUNCIATION Sentence stress

▶ **A** Listen and practice. Notice that the important words in a sentence have more stress.

● ●
Let's see . . .

● ● ●
Excuse me.
I'll take it.

● ● ● ●
That's expensive.
Can I help you?

● ● ● ●
Do you mean these?

B PAIR WORK Practice the conversations in Exercise 3, part B again. Pay attention to the sentence stress.

5 ROLE PLAY Can I help you?

A PAIR WORK Put items "for sale" on your desk, such as notebooks, watches, phones, or bags.

Student A: You are a salesclerk. Answer the customer's questions.

Student B: You are a customer. Ask the price of each item. Say if you want to buy it.

A: Can I help you?
B: Yes. I like this pen. How much is it?
A: Which one?

B Change roles and try the role play again.

6 LISTENING Wow! It's expensive!

▶ **A** Listen to two friends shopping. Write the color and price for each item.

	1. tablet	2. headphones	3. sunglasses	4. T-shirt
color				
price				
Do they buy it?	☐ Yes ☐ No	☐ Yes ☐ No	☐ Yes ☐ No	☐ Yes ☐ No

▶ **B** Listen again. Do they buy the items? Check (✓) Yes or No.

7 INTERCHANGE 3 Flea market

See what kinds of deals you can make as a buyer and a seller.
Go to Interchange 3 on pages 116–117.

8 WORD POWER Materials

A What are these things made of? Label each one. Use the words from the list.

| cotton | gold | leather | plastic | rubber | silk | silver | wool |

1. a ___silk___ tie
2. a _____ bracelet
3. a _____ ring
4. a _____ shirt
5. a _____ belt
6. _____ earrings
7. _____ flip-flops
8. _____ socks

B **PAIR WORK** What other materials are the things in part A sometimes made of? Make a list.

C **CLASS ACTIVITY** Which materials can you find in your classroom?
"Min-hee has gold earrings, and Ray has a leather jacket."

9 CONVERSATION That's a good point.

A Listen and practice.

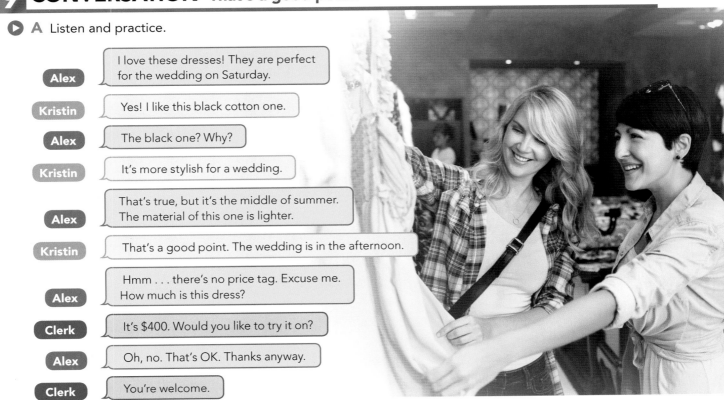

Alex I love these dresses! They are perfect for the wedding on Saturday.

Kristin Yes! I like this black cotton one.

Alex The black one? Why?

Kristin It's more stylish for a wedding.

Alex That's true, but it's the middle of summer. The material of this one is lighter.

Kristin That's a good point. The wedding is in the afternoon.

Alex Hmm . . . there's no price tag. Excuse me. How much is this dress?

Clerk It's $400. Would you like to try it on?

Alex Oh, no. That's OK. Thanks anyway.

Clerk You're welcome.

B Listen to the rest of the conversation. What does Alex buy? What does Kristin think of it?

10 GRAMMAR FOCUS

▶ Preferences; comparisons with adjectives

Which dress do you **prefer**?

  I **prefer** the blue one.   It's **nicer than** the black one.

Which one do you **like more**?

  I **like** the blue one **more**.   It's **lighter than** the black one.

Which one do you **like better**?

  I **like** the black one **better**.   It's **more stylish than** the blue one.

Spelling

cheap ⟶ cheap**er**

nice ⟶ nic**er**

big ⟶ bi**gger**

pretty ⟶ prett**ier**

GRAMMAR PLUS *see page 134*

A Complete these conversations. Then practice with a partner.

1. A: Which of these jackets do you like more?

   B: I prefer the leather one. The design is _____ (nice), and it looks _____ (expensive) the wool one.

2. A: These sweaters are nice. Which one do you prefer?

   B: I like the gray one better. The color is _____ (pretty). It's _____ (attractive) the brown and orange one.

3. A: Which rings do you like better?

   B: I like the silver ones more. They're _____ (small) the gold ones. And they're _____ (cheap).

B **PAIR WORK** Compare the things in part A. Give your own opinions.

  A: Which jacket do you like more?

  B: I like the wool one better. The color is prettier.

useful expressions

The color is prettier.

The design is nicer.

The style is more attractive.

The material is better.

11 WRITING My favorite clothes

A What do you like to wear? Write about your favorite clothes and compare them to clothes you don't like as much.

> My favorite clothes are cotton T-shirts and jeans. T-shirts are more comfortable than shirts and ties, and I think jeans are nicer than pants. I know that suits are more stylish, but . . .

B **GROUP WORK** Take turns reading your descriptions. Ask questions to get more information.

12 READING

A Skim the article. Why do you think people shop online?

● ● ● ‹ ›

Home	Posts	Archives	

ONLINE SHOPPING: The Crazy Things People Buy

In this week's blog, we look at some extraordinary things people can buy online.

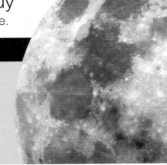

❶ A PIECE OF THE MOON: $27.50

It's true. You can own a piece of land on the moon. An acre, or about 4,000 square meters, of moon costs $27.50. That's a lot of space for your stuff. In fact, the price of each acre goes down when you buy more land. Imagine what you could do with all that space . . . if you could travel there! But don't worry, you get a certificate that says the land is yours.

❷ SOMEONE TO STAND IN LINE FOR YOU: $25 AN HOUR

No one likes to stand in line, right? Now you don't have to! For $25 an hour, someone waits patiently in line to get the stuff you need. Imagine that! Some people pay for someone to stand in line for movie tickets or for a new video game that's on sale. Make a reservation online in just a few clicks.

❸ SOME VERY EXPENSIVE SNEAKERS: $20,000 AND UP

Do you ever think your shoes are boring? Well, our sneakers are just what you need. Just go to our online store, look for a pair of sneakers you like, and place a bid. Maybe you'll win! Some of the sneakers are from famous basketball players.

❹ NO TIME FOR A REAL PET: $12

Many people like dogs and cats, but they just don't have the time to take care of them. If that sounds like you, here's the answer to your problem: a digital pet rock. It's clean, it's quiet, and it doesn't need food. It comes in a box. We think it's just about the perfect pet. You plug it into your laptop, and it's always with you!

B Read the blog. Find the item and write its name. Then write the number of the paragraph where you find the answers.

Find something . . .

a. . . . that you can wear. _____

b. . . . that you use with your laptop. _____

c. . . . that saves you a lot of time. _____

d. . . . that is huge. _____

C **GROUP WORK** The person who invented the first pet rock, Gary Dahl, became a millionaire. Why do you think people bought pet rocks? Do you think Mr. Dahl was a smart man? Would you buy a pet rock? Would you buy any of the other things? How much would you spend? Tell your classmates.

4 Do you play the guitar?

▶ Discuss entertainment likes and dislikes
▶ Make, accept, and decline invitations

1 SNAPSHOT

MUSIC SALES
IN THE UNITED STATES

Country 11.2%
Electronic 3.4%
Latin 2.6%
Classical 1.4%
Jazz 1.4%
Rock 29%
Pop 14.9%
R&B and Hip-Hop 17.2%
Other 18.4%

What styles of music do you like? What styles do you dislike?
What styles of music are popular in your country?

2 WORD POWER That's entertainment!

A Complete the word map with words from the list. Some words can go in more than one category.

action   reality show
electronic   reggae
game show   salsa
horror   science fiction
musical   soap opera
rap   talk show

ENTERTAINMENT

TV SHOWS

MOVIES

MUSIC

B Add two more words to each category. Then compare with a partner.

C GROUP WORK Number the items in each list from 1 (you like it the most) to 6 (you like it the least). Then compare your ideas.

3 CONVERSATION What kind of music do you like?

▶ **A** Listen and practice.

 LEANNE I can't wait for the Taylor Swift concert this Friday!

 SETH I think I know her. Does she play the violin?

 LEANNE No. She's a pop star.

 SETH Of course! I guess I don't listen to pop music a lot.

 LEANNE Oh, really? What kind of music do you like?

 SETH I really like hip-hop. Drake is my favorite musician.

 LEANNE Doesn't Drake play the guitar?

 SETH No, Leanne. He sings and raps.

 LEANNE OK. Well, I think we need to teach each other about music!

▶ **B** Listen to the rest of the conversation. Who is Seth's favorite band? Does Leanne like them?

4 GRAMMAR FOCUS

▶ **Simple present questions; short answers**

		Object pronouns
Do you **like** country music? Yes, I **do**. I love it. No, I **don't**. I don't like it very much.	What kind of music **do** you **like**? I really like rap.	me
		you
Does she **play** the piano? Yes, she **does**. She plays very well. No, she **doesn't**. She doesn't play an instrument.	**What does** she **play**? She plays the guitar.	him
		her
		it
Do they **like** Imagine Dragons? Yes, they **do**. They like them a lot. No, they **don't**. They don't like them at all.	**Who do** they **like**? They like Maroon 5.	us
		them

GRAMMAR PLUS *see page 135*

Complete these conversations. Then practice with a partner.

1. **A:** I like Alabama Shakes a lot. _____ you know _____?
   B: Yes, I _____, and I love this song. Let's download _____.
2. **A:** _____ you like science fiction movies?
   B: Yes, I _____. I like _____ very much.
3. **A:** _____ Vinnie and Midori like soap operas?
   B: Vinnie _____, but Midori _____. She hates _____.
4. **A:** What kind of music _____ Maya like?
   B: Classical music. She loves Yo-Yo Ma.
   A: Yeah, he's amazing. I like _____ a lot.

Alabama Shakes

5 PRONUNCIATION Intonation in questions

▶ **A** Listen and practice. Yes/No questions usually have rising intonation.
Wh-questions usually have falling intonation.

Do you like pop music?   What kind of music do you like?

B PAIR WORK Practice these questions.

Do you like TV?	What shows do you like?
Do you like video games?	What games do you like?
Do you play a musical instrument?	What instrument do you play?

6 SPEAKING Entertainment survey

A GROUP WORK Write five questions about entertainment and entertainers.
Then ask and answer your questions in groups.

What kinds of . . . do you like?
   (music, TV shows, video games)
Do you like . . . ?
   (reggae, game shows, action movies)
Who's your favorite . . . ?
   (singer, actor, athlete)

B GROUP WORK Complete this information about your group.
Ask any additional questions.

Our group FAVORITES

What's your favorite kind of . . . ?

music _____
movie _____
TV show _____

What's your favorite . . . ?

song _____
movie _____
video game _____

Who's your favorite . . . ?

singer _____
actor _____
athlete _____

Adele

Steph Curry

Star Wars: The Force Awakens

Top Chef

C CLASS ACTIVITY Read your group's list to the class.
Find out the class favorites.

7 LISTENING The perfect date

▶ **A** Listen to a host and four people on a TV game show. Three men want to invite Alexis on a date. What kinds of things do they like? Complete the chart.

	Jacob	Tyler	Andrew	Alexis
Music				
Movies				
TV shows				

B CLASS ACTIVITY Who do you think is the best date for Alexis? Why?

8 CONVERSATION What time does it start?

▶ **A** Listen and practice.

CONNOR I have tickets to my brother's concert on Friday night. Would you like to go?

CAMILA Thanks, I'd love to. What time does it start?

CONNOR At 8:00.

CAMILA Do you want to have dinner before? Maybe at 6:00?

CONNOR Well, I'd like to, but I have to work late. Let's just meet before the concert, around 7:30.

CAMILA No problem. We can have dinner another day. Let's meet at your office and go together.

CONNOR Sounds good! See you on Friday.

▶ **B** Listen to Connor and Camila talking at the concert. Does Camila like the concert? Does Connor's brother play well?

9 GRAMMAR FOCUS

Would; verb + to + verb

		Contractions
Would you **like to go** out on Friday?	**Would** you **like to go** to a concert?	**I'd** = I would
Yes, I **would**.	**I'd like to**, but I **have to work** late.	
Yes, **I'd love to**. Thanks.	**I'd like to**, but I **need to save** money.	
	I'd like to, but I **want to visit** my parents.	

GRAMMAR PLUS *see page 135*

A Respond to three invitations. Then write three invitations for the given responses.

1. **A:** I have tickets to the soccer game on Sunday. Would you like to go?

   B: _____

2. **A:** Would you like to come over for dinner tomorrow night?

   B: _____

3. **A:** Would you like to go to a hip-hop dance class with me this weekend?

   B: _____

4. **A:** _____
   _____

   B: Yes, I'd love to. Thank you!

5. **A:** _____
   _____

   B: Well, I'd like to, but I have to study.

6. **A:** _____
   _____

   B: Yes, I would. I really like electronic music.

B **PAIR WORK** Ask and answer the questions in part A. Give your own responses.

C **PAIR WORK** Think of three things you would like to do. Then invite a partner to do them with you. Your partner responds and asks follow-up questions like these:

When is it?   Where is it?   What time does it start?   When does it end?

10 WRITING Text messages

A What do these text messages say?

text message abbreviations	
u = you	afaik = as far as I know
r = are	lol = laugh out loud
2 = to / too	idk = I don't know
pls = please	msg = message
thx = thanks	nm = never mind
imo = in my opinion	brb = be right back
tbh = to be honest	ttyl = talk to you later

B **GROUP WORK** Write a "text message" to each person in your group. Then exchange messages. Write a response to each message.

11 INTERCHANGE 4 Are you free this weekend?

Make weekend plans with your classmates. Go to Interchange 4 on page 118.

12 READING

A Scan the article and look at the pictures. In what year did each event take place?

The World's Most Powerful
FEMALE MUSICIAN

Beyoncé Knowles-Carter is a singer, songwriter, performer, actress, clothing designer, and Grammy Award–winning superstar. Many people call her one of the most powerful female musicians in history. Beyoncé works really hard for her success. As she says, "I wanted to sell a million records, and I sold a million records. I wanted to go platinum; I went platinum. I've been working nonstop since I was 15. I don't even know how to chill out."

Many people talk about Beyoncé's energy on stage. She's an amazing entertainer. Millions of fans love her singing and dancing. Beyoncé uses many different styles of music, including funk, soul, and pop. In her career so far, Beyoncé has sold over 100 million records as a solo artist and another 60 million records with her group Destiny's Child.

Beyoncé marries Jay-Z.

Beyoncé performs at the U.S. president's inauguration.

BEYONCÉ FAST FACTS

1981	Beyoncé is born in Houston, Texas.
1996	Her girl group, Destiny's Child, gets its first recording contract.
2001	Beyoncé experiences her first time acting. She stars in *Carmen: A Hip Hopera* on MTV.
2003	She releases her first solo album, *Dangerously in Love*.
2004	She wins five Grammys at the Grammy Awards.
2005	Beyoncé starts an organization to help hurricane victims.
2008	She marries rapper Jay-Z.
2010	She wins six Grammys at the Grammy Awards for her album *I Am . . . Sasha Fierce*.
2012	Beyoncé has a daughter and names her Blue Ivy.
2013	Beyoncé performs at the U.S. president's inauguration.
2013	She releases a secret album online named *Beyoncé*.
2016	Beyoncé performs her song "Formation" at a huge sporting event.

B Read the article. Then number these sentences from 1 (first event) to 8 (last event).

_____ **a.** She performs at a president's inauguration.

_____ **b.** She is born in Texas.

_____ **c.** She acts in a movie.

_____ **d.** She wins five Grammys.

_____ **e.** She releases her first solo album.

_____ **f.** She has a baby.

_____ **g.** Her group gets its first recording contract.

_____ **h.** She helps hurricane victims.

C **PAIR WORK** Who is your favorite musician? What do you know about his or her life?

Units 3–4 Progress check

SELF-ASSESSMENT

How well can you do these things? Check (✓) the boxes.

I can . . .	Very well	OK	A little
Give and understand information about prices (Ex. 1)	☐	☐	☐
Say what I like and dislike (Ex. 1, 2, 3)	☐	☐	☐
Explain why I like or dislike something (Ex. 2)	☐	☐	☐
Describe and compare objects and possessions (Ex. 2)	☐	☐	☐
Make and respond to invitiations (Ex. 4)	☐	☐	☐

1 LISTENING Price Cut City

▶ **A** Listen to a commercial for Price Cut City. Choose the correct prices.

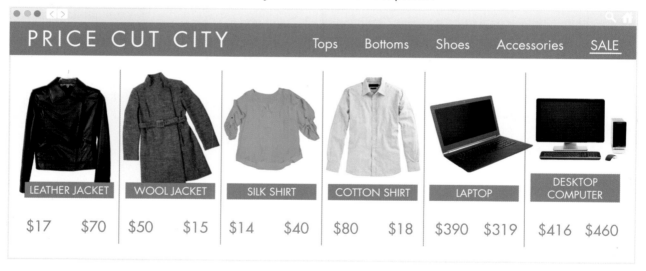

B PAIR WORK What do you think of the items in part A? At what stores or websites can you find items like these at low prices? Give your own ideas and opinions.

2 ROLE PLAY Shopping trip

Student A: Choose things from Exercise 1 for your family. Ask for Student B's opinion.
Student B: Help Student A choose presents for his or her family.

> **A:** I want to buy a laptop for my parents. Which one do you like better?
> **B:** Well, I like . . . better. It's nicer, and . . .

Change roles and try the role play again.

3 SPEAKING Survey: Likes and dislikes

A Add one more question to the chart. Write your answers to these questions.

	Me	My classmate
When do you usually watch TV?		
What kinds of TV shows do you like?		
Do you like game shows?		
Do you read the news online?		
Who is your favorite singer?		
What do you think of hip-hop?		
What is your favorite movie?		
Do you like musicals?		
What kinds of movies do you dislike?		

B **CLASS ACTIVITY** Go around the class. Find someone who has the same answers as you. Write a classmate's name only once!

4 SPEAKING What an excuse!

A Make up three invitations to interesting activities. Write them on cards.

> My friends and I are going to the
> amusement park on Sunday at
> 2 p.m. Would you like to come?

B Write three response cards. One is an acceptance card, and two are refusals. Think of silly or unusual excuses.

> That sounds great! What
> time do you want to meet?

> I'd like to, but I have to wash
> my cat tomorrow.

> I'd love to, but I want to take
> my bird to a singing contest.

C **GROUP WORK** Shuffle the invitation cards together and the response cards together. Take three cards from each pile. Then invite people to do the things on your invitation cards. Use the response cards to accept or refuse.

WHAT'S NEXT?

Look at your Self-assessment again. Do you need to review anything?

5 What an interesting family!

▶ Describe families
▶ Talk about habitual and current activities

1 WORD POWER Family

A Look at Joseph's family tree. How are these people related to him? Add the words to the family tree.

cousin   niece
daughter   sister-in-law
father   uncle
grandmother   wife

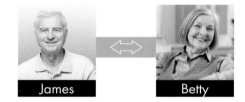

James ⟷ Betty

grandfather and _____

Robert ⟷ Patricia   Deborah ⟷ Arturo

_____ and mother   aunt and _____

Joseph ⟷ Keiko   Joshua ⟷ Nicole   Veronica

Joseph (husband) and his _____   brother and _____   _____

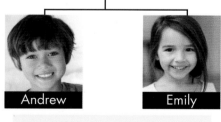   

Andrew   Emily   Alyssa   Ethan

son and _____   _____ and nephew

B Draw your family tree (or a friend's family tree). Then take turns talking about your families. Ask follow-up questions to get more information.

A: There are six people in my family. I have one brother and two sisters.
B: How old is your brother?

2 LISTENING Famous relatives

▶ Listen to four conversations about famous people. How is the second person related to the first person?

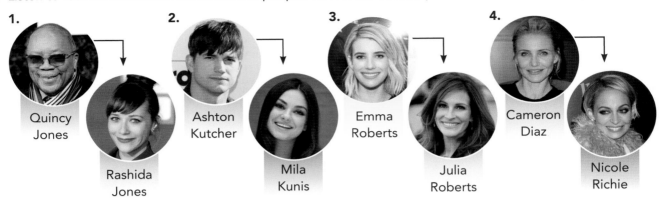

1. Quincy Jones → Rashida Jones
2. Ashton Kutcher → Mila Kunis
3. Emma Roberts → Julia Roberts
4. Cameron Diaz → Nicole Richie

3 CONVERSATION He's traveling in Thailand.

▶ **A** Listen and practice.

	MAX	Do you have brothers and sisters, Tina?
	TINA	Yes, I have a brother and a sister.
	MAX	Oh, what does your sister do?
	TINA	She's a surgeon. She works for a medical aid organization.
	MAX	Wow! And what about your brother?
	TINA	He's a writer. He travels and writes about his experiences for a magazine.
	MAX	What an interesting family! Can I meet them?
	TINA	Sure, but my sister's not here right now. She's treating patients in Cameroon.
	MAX	And your brother?
	TINA	He's traveling in Thailand, and then he wants to visit my sister. I miss them!

▶ **B** Listen to the rest of the conversation. Where do Max's parents live? What do his parents do?

4 PRONUNCIATION Intonation in statements

▶ **A** Listen and practice. Notice that statements usually have falling intonation.

She's working in Cameroon.   He's traveling in Thailand.

B PAIR WORK Practice the conversation in Exercise 3 again.

5 GRAMMAR FOCUS

▶ **Present continuous**

Are you **living** at home now?	Yes, I **am**.	No, I**'m not**.
Is your sister **working** in another city?	Yes, she **is**.	No, she**'s not**./No, she **isn't**.
Are your parents **studying** English this year?	Yes, they **are**.	No, they**'re not**./No, they **aren't**.

Where **are** you **working** now?	I**'m not working**. I need a job.
What **is** your brother **doing**?	He**'s traveling** in Thailand.
What **are** your friends **doing** these days?	They**'re studying** for their exams.

GRAMMAR PLUS *see page 136*

A Complete these phone conversations using the present continuous.

A: Hi, Brittany. What _____ you _____ (do)?

B: Hey, Zach. I _____ (eat) a sandwich at O'Connor's.

A: Mmm! Is it good?

B: Yeah. It's delicious. Wait, they _____ (bring) my dessert now. It's chocolate cake with ice cream. Call you later! Bye!

A: So, Madison, how _____ you and your sister _____ (do) in college?

B: We _____ (have) a lot of fun, Mom!

A: Fun? OK, but _____ your sister _____ (go) to class every morning?

B: Yeah, Mom. She _____ (work) hard and I am, too. I'm serious!

B PAIR WORK Write a short dialogue using the present continuous, then practice it.

C CLASS WORK Read your dialogue to the class.

6 DISCUSSION What are you doing these days?

GROUP WORK Ask and answer questions about what you are doing. Use the topics in the box and your own ideas. Ask follow-up questions to get more information.

A: So, what are you doing these days?

B: I'm playing basketball in college.

A: That's nice. And are you enjoying it?

topics to talk about	
traveling	going to high school or college
playing a sport	learning a musical instrument
living alone	working or studying

7 INTERCHANGE 5 Is that true?

Find out about your classmates' families. Go to Interchange 5 on page 119.

8 SNAPSHOT

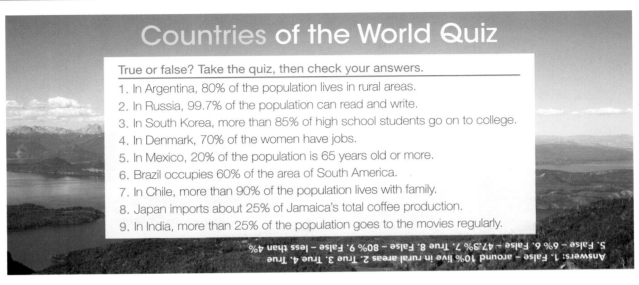

Countries of the World Quiz

True or false? Take the quiz, then check your answers.

1. In Argentina, 80% of the population lives in rural areas.
2. In Russia, 99.7% of the population can read and write.
3. In South Korea, more than 85% of high school students go on to college.
4. In Denmark, 70% of the women have jobs.
5. In Mexico, 20% of the population is 65 years old or more.
6. Brazil occupies 60% of the area of South America.
7. In Chile, more than 90% of the population lives with family.
8. Japan imports about 25% of Jamaica's total coffee production.
9. In India, more than 25% of the population goes to the movies regularly.

Answers: 1. False – around 10% live in rural areas 2. True 3. True 4. True 5. False – 6% 6. False – 47.3% 7. True 8. False – 80% 9. False – less than 4%

Which facts surprise you? Why?
What interesting facts do you know about your country?

9 CONVERSATION I didn't know that.

▶ **A** Listen and practice.

 LUIS What a great picture! Are those your parents?

 VICKY Thanks! Yes, it's my favorite picture of us.

 LUIS It's really nice. So, do you have any brothers or sisters?

 VICKY No, I'm an only child. Actually, a lot of families in China have only one child.

 LUIS Oh, really? I didn't know that.

 VICKY What about you, Luis?

 LUIS I come from a big family. I have two brothers and four sisters.

 VICKY Wow! Is that typical in Peru?

 LUIS I'm not sure. Many families are smaller these days. But big families are great because you get a lot of birthday presents!

▶ **B** Listen to the rest of the conversation. What does Vicky like about being an only child?

What an interesting family! **33**

▶ Quantifiers

100%	**All**	
	Nearly all	families have only one child.
	Most	
	Many	
	A lot of	families are smaller these days.
	Some	
	Not many	couples have more than one child.
	Few	
0%	**No one**	gets married before the age of 18.

GRAMMAR PLUS *see page 136*

A Rewrite these sentences using quantifiers. Then compare with a partner.

1. In the U.S., 69% of high school students go to college.
   _____

2. Seven percent of the people in Brazil are age 65 or older.
   _____

3. In India, 0% of the people vote before the age of 18.
   _____

4. Forty percent of the people in Sweden live alone.
   _____

5. In Canada, 22% of the people speak French at home.
   _____

B **PAIR WORK** Rewrite the sentences in part A so that they are true about your country.

> In the U.S., most high school students go to college.

11 WRITING An email to an online friend

A You have an online friend in another country. Write an email to your friend about your family.

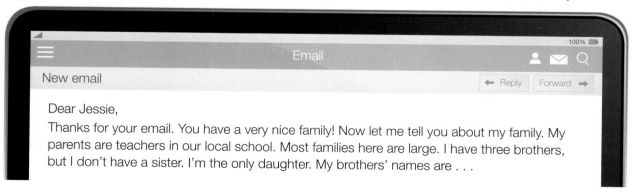

Email

New email   ← Reply   Forward →

Dear Jessie,
Thanks for your email. You have a very nice family! Now let me tell you about my family. My parents are teachers in our local school. Most families here are large. I have three brothers, but I don't have a sister. I'm the only daughter. My brothers' names are . . .

B **GROUP WORK** Take turns reading your emails. Ask questions to get more information.

A A journalist interviewed four people. Read the title of the article. What do you think the answer will be? Check (✓) the answer.

☐ Yes, most families do. ☐ No, most families don't. ☐ Some families do, some families don't.

DO FAMILIES SPEND A LOT OF TIME TOGETHER?

We spend a lot of time together on the weekends. My husband and I always take our son, Oliver, and daughter, Samantha, out to do something fun. Some weeks we go for a long bike ride and get a lot of fresh air! We go to the beach in the summer, of course. In the evenings, we have a barbecue together. During the week, it's more difficult to spend time together because of work and school.
– *Jane Chambers*

It's a little sad, but most of the time we spend as a family is watching TV. We don't talk much. My mom and dad both work, and they're often tired when they get home. My sister just plays games on her tablet all evening. It's kind of boring. Maybe we spend about an hour a day together. It's never more than that.
– *Billy Foster*

I'm a stay-at-home dad, and I'm having a great time with my family! When the kids are in school, I do housework. When they come home, I help them with their homework. After that, we all have fun together. We play a lot of sports and read books. I love all the time I get with my two boys.
– *Nick Ramos*

We're always really busy, but we make an effort to spend time together. My grandparents come over to our house twice a week for dinner. I think family is very important. I often help my mom or dad cook the meals. Sometimes we all go to the movies. I like that a lot.
– *Carla Costantini*

B Read the interviews. Then check the correct names.

Who . . . ?	Jane	Billy	Nick	Carla
1. watches a lot of TV	☐	☐	☐	☐
2. sees their grandparents twice a week	☐	☐	☐	☐
3. spends time outdoors	☐	☐	☐	☐
4. stays at home with the kids	☐	☐	☐	☐
5. doesn't spend much time with family	☐	☐	☐	☐
6. does housework during the day	☐	☐	☐	☐

C **GROUP WORK** What do families look like in your country? Do dads stay at home with their children? Do you think that's a good thing or a bad thing? Is it important to you to spend time with your family?

6 How often do you run?

▶ Discuss sports and exercise habits
▶ Ask and answer questions about frequency of free-time activities

1 SNAPSHOT

Top Sports and Fitness Activities in the United States

Sports
- [ ] football
- [ ] baseball
- [ ] soccer
- [ ] ice hockey
- [ ] basketball

Fitness Activities
- [ ] treadmill
- [ ] running/jogging
- [ ] walking
- [ ] bowling
- [ ] weight training

Do people in your country enjoy any of these sports or activities?
Check (✓) the sports or fitness activities you enjoy.
Make a list of other activities you do. Then compare with the class.

2 WORD POWER Sports and fitness

A Which of these activities are popular with the following age groups in your country? Check (✓) the activities. Then compare with a partner.

	Children	Teens	Young adults	Middle-aged people	Older people
bike riding	[ ]	[ ]	[ ]	[ ]	[ ]
golf	[ ]	[ ]	[ ]	[ ]	[ ]
jogging	[ ]	[ ]	[ ]	[ ]	[ ]
martial arts	[ ]	[ ]	[ ]	[ ]	[ ]
Pilates	[ ]	[ ]	[ ]	[ ]	[ ]
soccer	[ ]	[ ]	[ ]	[ ]	[ ]
swimming	[ ]	[ ]	[ ]	[ ]	[ ]
volleyball	[ ]	[ ]	[ ]	[ ]	[ ]
yoga	[ ]	[ ]	[ ]	[ ]	[ ]

B PAIR WORK Which activities in part A are used with *do*, *go*, or *play*?

do martial arts   _go bike riding_   _play golf_

3 CONVERSATION I run every day.

▶ **A** Listen and practice.

Aaron: You have a lot of energy, Riley. Do you exercise a lot?

Riley: Well, I get up early and run on the treadmill for an hour every day.

Aaron: Seriously?

Riley: Sure. And I do weight lifting.

Aaron: Wow! How often do you lift weights?

Riley: I usually do it about three times a week. What about you?

Aaron: Oh, I hardly ever exercise. I usually just watch TV or listen to music in my free time. I guess I'm a real couch potato!

▶ **B** Listen to the rest of the conversation. What else does Riley do in her free time?

4 GRAMMAR FOCUS

▶ **Adverbs of frequency**

How often do you exercise?	Do you **ever** watch TV in the evening?	100% **always**
I run on the treadmill **every day**.	Yes, I **often** watch TV after dinner.	**almost always**
I go jogging **once a week**.	I **sometimes** watch TV before bed.	**usually**
I play soccer **twice a month**.	**Sometimes** I watch TV before bed.*	**often**
I swim about **three times a year**.	I **hardly ever** watch TV.	**sometimes**
I don't exercise very **often/much**.	No, I **never** watch TV.	**hardly ever**
Usually I exercise before class.*		**almost never**
*__Usually__ and **sometimes** can begin a sentence.*		0% **never**

GRAMMAR PLUS *see page 137*

A Put the adverbs in the correct place. Sometimes there is more than one correct answer. Then practice with a partner.

1. **A:** Do you play sports? (ever)
   B: Sure. I play soccer. (twice a week)
2. **A:** What do you do on Saturday mornings? (usually)
   B: Nothing much. I sleep until noon. (almost always)
3. **A:** Do you lift weights at the gym? (often)
   B: No, I lift weights. (hardly ever)
4. **A:** Do you exercise on Sundays? (always)
   B: No, I exercise on Sundays. (never)

5. **A:** What do you do after class? (usually)
   B: I go out with my classmates. (about three times a week)
6. **A:** Do you go to the movies? (often)
   B: Yes, I go to the movies. (once a week)
7. **A:** Do you go bike riding? (ever)
   B: No, I ride a bike. (hardly ever)
8. **A:** Do you walk to school? (sometimes)
   B: Sure. I walk to school. (five days a week)

B **PAIR WORK** Take turns asking the questions in part A. Give your own information when answering.

5 PRONUNCIATION Intonation with direct address

▶ **A** Listen and practice. Notice these statements with direct address.
There is usually falling intonation and a pause before the name.

You have a lot of energy, Riley.   You look tired, Aaron.   I feel great, Dr. Yun.

B PAIR WORK Write four statements using direct address. Then practice them.

6 SPEAKING Fitness programs

A GROUP WORK Take a poll in your group. Take turns asking each person these questions.
Each person gets two points for each *Yes* answer and one point for each *No* answer.

1	2	3	4	5
Do you have a regular fitness program? YES ☐ NO ☐ How often do you exercise?	Do you ever go to a gym? YES ☐ NO ☐ How often do you go? What do you do there?	Do you play any sports? YES ☐ NO ☐ Which ones? How often do you play them?	Do you ever take long walks? YES ☐ NO ☐ How often? Where do you go?	Do you do anything else to keep fit? YES ☐ NO ☐ What do you do?

B GROUP WORK Add up your points and study the results of the poll.
Who in your group got at least six points?

C CLASS WORK Tell the class about one of the people in your group.

"Cynthia does Pilates twice a week, and sometimes she goes jogging. She doesn't . . ."

7 LISTENING I swim twice a week.

▶ **A** Listen to three people discuss what they like to do in the evening.
Complete the chart.

	Activity	How often?
Joseph		
Victoria		
Carlos		

▶ **B** Listen again. Who is most similar to you – Joseph, Victoria, or Carlos?

8 DISCUSSION Olympic sports and athletes

GROUP WORK Take turns asking and answering these questions.

Can you remember the names of five Olympic sports?
    What are they?
Do you ever watch Olympic sports on TV? Which ones?
Would you like to see Olympic sports live? Why? Why not?
Do you prefer the summer or winter Olympics? Why?
What's your favorite Olympic sport? Why?
What's an Olympic sport that you really don't like? Why not?
Who's a famous male athlete in your country? What sport
    does he play?
Who's a famous female athlete? What sport does she play?

9 WRITING Your weekly activities

A Write about your weekly activities. Include your favorite activity, but don't say which one is your favorite.

> I usually *exercise four or five times a week*. I always do yoga on Mondays and Wednesdays. I often go jogging in the morning on Tuesdays and Thursdays. I sometimes go to the beach and play volleyball with my friends on weekends. I . . .

B **GROUP WORK** Take turns reading your descriptions. Can you guess your partners' favorite activities?
"Your favorite activity is volleyball, right?"

10 CONVERSATION You're in great shape.

▶ **A** Listen and practice.

 STEPH You're in great shape, Mick.

MICK Thanks. I guess I'm a real fitness freak.

 STEPH How often do you work out?

MICK Well, I go swimming and lift weights every day. And I play tennis three times a week.

STEPH Tennis? That sounds like a lot of fun.

MICK Oh, do you want to play sometime?

STEPH Uh . . . how well do you play?

MICK Pretty well, I guess.

STEPH Well, all right. But I'm not very good.

 MICK No problem. I'll give you a few tips.

▶ **B** Listen to Mick and Steph after their tennis match. Who's the winner?

11 GRAMMAR FOCUS

▶ Questions with *how*; short answers

How often do you work out?
    Every day.
    Twice a week.
    Not very often.

How long do you spend at the gym?
    Thirty minutes a day.
    Two hours a week.
    About an hour on weekends.

How well do you play tennis?
    Pretty well.
    About average.
    Not very well.

How good are you at sports?
    Pretty good.
    OK.
    Not so good.

GRAMMAR PLUS *see page 137*

A Complete these questions. Then practice with a partner.

1. **A:** _____ at sports?
   B: I guess I'm pretty good. I play a lot of different sports.
2. **A:** _____ spend online?
   B: About an hour after dinner. I like to chat with my friends.
3. **A:** _____ go to the beach?
   B: Once or twice a month. It's a good way to relax.
4. **A:** _____ swim?
   B: Not very well. I need to take swimming lessons.

B **GROUP WORK** Take turns asking the questions in part A. Give your own information when answering. Then ask more questions with *how often*, *how long*, *how well*, and *how good*.

12 LISTENING You're in great shape!

▶ Listen to Rachel, Nicholas, Zack, and Jennifer discuss sports and exercise. Who is a couch potato? a fitness freak? a sports nut? a gym rat?

a couch potato

a fitness freak

a sports nut

a gym rat

1. _____ 2. _____ 3. _____ 4. _____

13 INTERCHANGE 6 What's your talent?

Find out how well your classmates do different activities. Go to Interchange 6 on page 120.

A How healthy and fit do you think you are? Skim the questions. Then guess your health and fitness score from 0 (very unhealthy) to 50 (very healthy).

FIT AND HEALTHY?

Take the quiz!

1. **How many servings of fruits or vegetables do you eat each day?**

Five or more.	5
Between one and four.	3
I don't eat fruits or vegetables.	0

2. **How much sugar do you use in food and drinks?**

I hardly ever use sugar in my food and drink.	5
A little, but I'm careful.	3
A lot. I love sugar!	0

3. **How often do you eat junk food?**

Never.	5
Maybe once a week.	3
As often as possible.	0

4. **How many glasses of water do you drink each day?**

Eight or more.	5
Between one and three.	3
I almost always drink soda.	0

5. **Do you eat oily fish (for example, sardines, salmon)?**

Yes, I love fish!	5
Yes, about twice a month.	3
No, I really don't like fish.	0

6. **How often do you exercise?**

I usually exercise every day.	5
Two or three times a week.	3
What's exercise?	0

7. **Do you walk or bike to work or school?**

Yes, whenever I can.	5
I do when I have time.	3
No, never.	0

8. **Is fitness important to you?**

Yes, it's extremely important.	5
I think it's pretty important.	3
No, it's not important at all.	0

9. **What do you do on weekends?**

I play as many kinds of sports as I can!	5
I sometimes go for walks or bike rides.	3
I watch TV all day long.	0

10. **When you're at work or school, how active are you?**

Very active. I walk around a lot.	5
A little active. I go for a walk at lunchtime.	3
I sit at my desk and order lunch.	0

RATE YOURSELF!

42 to 50: Good job! You're doing all the right things for a healthy life.

28 to 41: You're on the right track. With a little more work, you'll be great.

15 to 27: Keep trying! You can be very fit and healthy, so don't give up!

14 or below: It's time to improve your health and fitness. You can do it!

B Take the quiz and add up your score. Is your score similar to your original guess? Do you agree with your score? Why or why not?

C **GROUP WORK** Compare your scores. Who is healthy and fit? What can your classmates do to improve their health and fitness?

SELF-ASSESSMENT

How well can you do these things? Check (✓) the boxes.

I can . . .	Very well	OK	A little
Ask about and describe present activities (Ex. 1, 2, 3)	☐	☐	☐
Describe family life (Ex. 3)	☐	☐	☐
Ask for and give personal information (Ex. 3)	☐	☐	☐
Give information about quantities (Ex. 3)	☐	☐	☐
Ask and answer questions about free time (Ex. 4)	☐	☐	☐
Ask and answer questions about routines and abilities (Ex. 4)	☐	☐	☐

1 LISTENING What are they doing?

▶ **A** Listen to people do different things.
What are they doing? Complete the chart.

B PAIR WORK Compare your answers.

A: In number one, someone is watching TV.
B: I don't think so. I think someone is . . .

> **What are they doing?**
> 1. _____
> 2. _____
> 3. _____
> 4. _____

2 SPEAKING Memory game

GROUP WORK Choose a person in the room, but don't say who! Other students ask yes/no questions to guess the person.

A: I'm thinking of someone in the classroom.
B: Is it a man?
A: Yes, it is.
C: Is he sitting in the front of the room?
A: No, he isn't.
D: Is he sitting in the back?
A: Yes, he is.
E: Is he wearing a black T-shirt?
A: No, he isn't.
B: Is it . . . ?

The student with the correct guess has the next turn.

3 SPEAKING Family life survey

A GROUP WORK Add two more yes/no questions about family life to the chart. Then ask and answer the questions in groups. Write down the number of "yes" and "no" answers. (Remember to include yourself.)

	Number of "yes" answers	Number of "no" answers
1. Are you living with your family?		
2. Do your parents both work?		
3. Do you eat dinner with your family?		
4. Are you exercising these days?		
5. Are you studying something these days?		
6. Do you have brothers or sisters?		
7. _____		
8. _____		

B GROUP WORK Write up the results of the survey. Then tell the class.

1. In our group, most people are living with their families.
2. Nearly all of our mothers and fathers work.

Quantifiers	
All	100%
Nearly all	
Most	
Many	
A lot of	
Some	
Not many	
Few	
No one	0%

4 DISCUSSION Routines and abilities

GROUP WORK Choose three questions. Then ask your questions in groups. When someone answers "yes," think of more questions to ask.

Do you ever . . . ?

☐ cook for friends
☐ do yoga
☐ go jogging

☐ listen to English songs
☐ play video games
☐ play volleyball

☐ sing in the shower
☐ tell jokes
☐ write emails in English

A: Do you ever cook for friends?
B: Yes, I often do.
C: What do you cook?
B: I usually cook fish or pasta.
A: When do you cook?
B: On weekends.
C: How often do you cook?
B: Once a month.
A: How well do you cook?
B: About average. But they always ask for more!

WHAT'S NEXT?

Look at your Self-assessment again. Do you need to review anything?

7 We went dancing!

▸ Describe past daily and free-time activities
▸ Describe past vacations

1 SNAPSHOT

Free-time Activities

- ☐ check social media
- ☐ go dancing
- ☐ listen to music
- ☐ play video games
- ☐ read
- ☐ relax
- ☐ spend time with friends and family
- ☐ watch TV

Check (✓) the activities you do in your free time. List three other activities you do in your free time. What are your favorite free-time activities? Are there activities you don't like? Which ones?

2 CONVERSATION What did you do last weekend?

▶ **A** Listen and practice.

NEIL So, what did you do last weekend, Cara?

CARA Oh, I had a great time. My friends and I had pizza on Saturday and then we all went dancing.

NEIL How fun! Did you go to The Treadmill?

CARA No, we didn't. We went to that new place downtown. How about you? Did you go anywhere?

NEIL No, I didn't go anywhere all weekend. I just stayed home and studied for today's Spanish test.

CARA Our test is today? I forgot about that!

NEIL Don't worry. You always get an A.

▶ **B** Listen to the rest of the conversation. What does Cara do on Sunday afternoons?

3 GRAMMAR FOCUS

▶ Simple past

Did you **work** on Saturday?
   Yes, I **did**. I **worked** all day.
   No, I **didn't**. I **didn't work** at all.

Did you **go** anywhere last weekend?
   Yes, I **did**. I **went** to the movies.
   No, I **didn't**. I **didn't go** anywhere.

What **did** Neil **do** on Saturday?
   He **stayed** home and **studied** for a test.

How **did** Cara **spend** her weekend?
   She **went** to a club and **danced** with some friends.

GRAMMAR PLUS *see page 138*

A Complete these conversations. Then practice with a partner.

1. A: _____ you _____ (stay) home on Sunday?
   B: No, I _____ (call) my friend Anna. We _____ (drive) to a nice little restaurant for lunch.

2. A: How _____ you _____ (spend) your last birthday?
   B: I _____ (have) a party. Everyone _____ (enjoy) it, but the neighbors next door _____ (not, like) the noise.

3. A: What _____ you _____ (do) last night?
   B: I _____ (see) a sci-fi movie at the Cineplex. I _____ (love) it! Amazing special effects!

4. A: _____ you _____ (do) anything special over the weekend?
   B: Yes, I _____. I _____ (go) shopping. Unfortunately, I _____ (spend) all my money. Now I'm broke!

5. A: _____ you _____ (go) out on Friday night?
   B: No, I _____. I _____ (invite) friends over, and I _____ (cook) spaghetti for them.

regular verbs

work ⟶ work**ed**
invite ⟶ invite**d**
study ⟶ stud**ied**
stop ⟶ stop**ped**

irregular verbs

buy ⟶ **bought**
do ⟶ **did**
drive ⟶ **drove**
have ⟶ **had**
go ⟶ **went**
sing ⟶ **sang**
see ⟶ **saw**
spend ⟶ **spent**

B **PAIR WORK** Take turns asking the questions in part A. Give your own information when answering.

   A: Did you stay home on Sunday?
   B: No, I didn't. I went dancing with some friends.

4 PRONUNCIATION Reduction of *did you*

▶ **A** Listen and practice. Notice how **did you** is reduced in the following questions.

   [dɪdʒə]
   Did you have a good time?

   [wədɪdʒə]
   What did you do last night?

   [haʊdɪdʒə]
   How did you like the movie?

B **PAIR WORK** Practice the questions in Exercise 3, part A again. Pay attention to the pronunciation of **did you**.

5 WORD POWER Chores and activities

A **PAIR WORK** Find two other words or phrases from the list that usually go with each verb. Then add one more word or phrase to each verb.

| a lot of fun | dancing | a good time | shopping | a bike ride |
| the bed | chores | the laundry | a trip | a video |

do	my homework			
go	online			
have	a party			
make	a phone call			
take	a day off			

B **GROUP WORK** Choose the things you did last weekend. Then compare with your partners.

A: I went shopping with my friends. We had a good time. What about you?
B: I didn't have a very good time. I did chores.
C: I did chores, too. But I went dancing in the evening, and . . .

6 DISCUSSION Ask some questions!

GROUP WORK Take turns. One student makes a statement about the weekend. Other students ask questions. Each student answers at least three questions.

A: I went shopping on Saturday afternoon.
B: **Where** did you go?
A: To the Mayfair Center.
C: **Who** did you go with?
A: I went with my friends and my sister.
D: **What time** did you go?
A: We went around 3:00.

7 LISTENING Did you have a good holiday?

▶ **A** Listen to Andrew tell Elizabeth what he did yesterday. Check (✓) the things Andrew did.

Activities	Reasons
☐ went to the gym	
☐ played soccer	
☐ saw a movie	
☐ watched TV	
☐ went to a baseball game	
☐ spent time with family	

▶ **B** Listen again. Look at the activities Andrew didn't do. Why didn't he do them? Write the reason.

Play a board game. Go to Interchange 7 on page 121.

9 CONVERSATION Lucky you!

▶ **A** Listen and practice.

Leah: Hi, Cody. How was your vacation?

Cody: It was excellent! I went to California with my cousin. We had a great time.

Leah: Lucky you! How long were you there?

Cody: About a week.

Leah: Cool! Was the weather OK?

Cody: Not really. It was pretty cloudy. But we went surfing every day. The waves were amazing.

Leah: So, what was the best thing about the trip?

Cody: Well, something incredible happened. . . .

▶ **B** Listen to the rest of the conversation. What happened?

10 GRAMMAR FOCUS

▶ **Past of be**

		Contractions
Were you in California?	Yes, I **was**.	wasn't = was **not**
Was the weather OK?	No, it **wasn't**.	weren't = were **not**
Were you and your cousin on vacation?	Yes, we **were**.	
Were your parents there?	No, they **weren't**.	
How long **were** you away?	I **was** away for a week.	
How **was** your vacation?	It **was** excellent!	

GRAMMAR PLUS *see page 138*

Complete these conversations. Then practice with a partner.

1. **A:** _____ you in New York last weekend?
   B: No, I _____. I _____ in Chicago.
   A: How _____ it?
   B: It _____ great! But it _____ cold and windy as usual.

2. **A:** How long _____ your parents in Chile?
   B: They _____ there for two weeks.
   A: _____ they in Santiago the whole time?
   B: No, they _____. They also went to Valparaiso.

3. **A:** _____ you away last week?
   B: Yes, I _____ in Madrid.
   A: Really? How long _____ you there?
   B: For almost a week. I _____ there on business.

11 DISCUSSION Past and future vacations

A GROUP WORK Ask your classmates about their last vacations.
Ask these questions or use your own ideas.

Where did you spend your last vacation?
How long was your vacation?
Who were you with?

What did you do?
How was the weather?
What would you like to do on
   your next vacation?

B CLASS ACTIVITY Who had an interesting vacation?
Tell the class who and why.

12 WRITING A blog post

A Read the blog post.

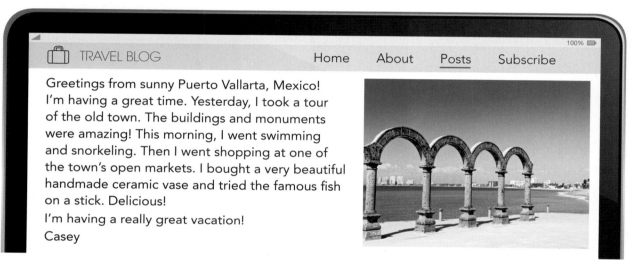

TRAVEL BLOG   Home   About   Posts   Subscribe

Greetings from sunny Puerto Vallarta, Mexico!
I'm having a great time. Yesterday, I took a tour
of the old town. The buildings and monuments
were amazing! This morning, I went swimming
and snorkeling. Then I went shopping at one of
the town's open markets. I bought a very beautiful
handmade ceramic vase and tried the famous fish
on a stick. Delicious!
I'm having a really great vacation!
Casey

B PAIR WORK Write a blog post to your partner about your last vacation. Then exchange posts.
Do you have any questions about your partner's vacation?

13 LISTENING I was on vacation.

A Listen to Daniel and Amanda talk about their vacations.
Did they have a good time? Check (✓) Yes or No.

	Yes	No
Daniel	☐	☐
Amanda	☐	☐

B Listen again. Complete the chart with information about their vacations.

Daniel's vacation		Amanda's vacation	
Place		Place	
Who with		Who with	
Activities		Activities	

A Look at the pictures. What do you think each person did on his or her vacation?

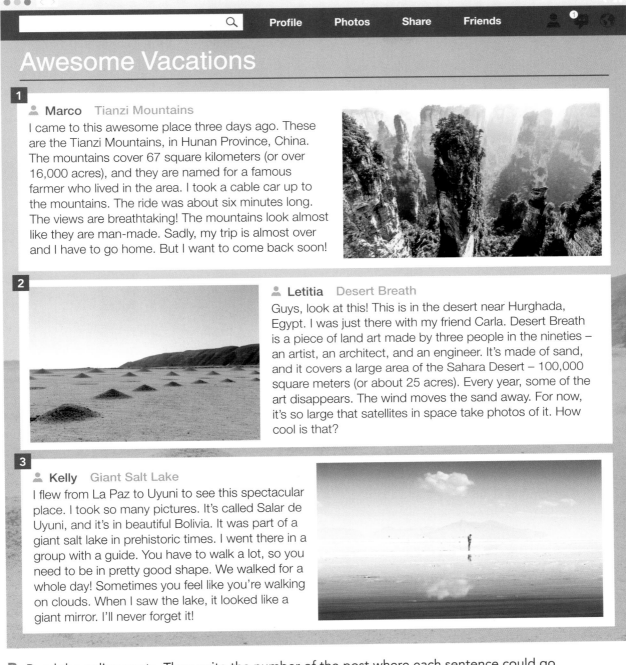

Awesome Vacations

1

Marco Tianzi Mountains

I came to this awesome place three days ago. These are the Tianzi Mountains, in Hunan Province, China. The mountains cover 67 square kilometers (or over 16,000 acres), and they are named for a famous farmer who lived in the area. I took a cable car up to the mountains. The ride was about six minutes long. The views are breathtaking! The mountains look almost like they are man-made. Sadly, my trip is almost over and I have to go home. But I want to come back soon!

2

Letitia Desert Breath

Guys, look at this! This is in the desert near Hurghada, Egypt. I was just there with my friend Carla. Desert Breath is a piece of land art made by three people in the nineties – an artist, an architect, and an engineer. It's made of sand, and it covers a large area of the Sahara Desert – 100,000 square meters (or about 25 acres). Every year, some of the art disappears. The wind moves the sand away. For now, it's so large that satellites in space take photos of it. How cool is that?

3

Kelly Giant Salt Lake

I flew from La Paz to Uyuni to see this spectacular place. I took so many pictures. It's called Salar de Uyuni, and it's in beautiful Bolivia. It was part of a giant salt lake in prehistoric times. I went there in a group with a guide. You have to walk a lot, so you need to be in pretty good shape. We walked for a whole day! Sometimes you feel like you're walking on clouds. When I saw the lake, it looked like a giant mirror. I'll never forget it!

B Read the online posts. Then write the number of the post where each sentence could go.

_____ It was pretty tiring, but I enjoyed every minute of it.

_____ The ride was scary because we were so high up.

_____ I hope to meet the people who made it.

C **PAIR WORK** Answer these questions.

1. Which person used an unusual form of transportation?

2. Who saw a piece of art?

3. Who had a very active vacation?

4. Which place do you think is the most interesting? Why?

8 How's the neighborhood?

▶ Ask about and describe places
▶ Describe a neighborhood

1 WORD POWER Places and activities

A Match the places and the definitions. Then ask and answer the questions with a partner.

What's a . . . ?

1. clothing store _____
2. grocery store _____
3. hair salon _____
4. laundromat _____
5. newsstand _____
6. stadium _____
7. Wi-Fi hot spot _____

It's a place where you . . .

a. get food and small items for the home
b. can connect to the Internet
c. get a haircut
d. buy newspapers and magazines
e. see a game or a concert
f. find new fashions
g. wash and dry your clothes

B PAIR WORK Write definitions for these places.

| coffee shop | drugstore | gas station | library | post office |

It's a place where you drink coffee and tea and eat small meals. (coffee shop)

C GROUP WORK Read your definitions. Can your classmates guess the places?

2 CONVERSATION I just moved in.

▶ Listen and practice.

Greg: Excuse me! Hi, I'm your new neighbor, Greg. I just moved in.

Mrs. Cook: Oh. Yes?

Greg: I'm looking for a grocery store. Are there any around here?

Mrs. Cook: Yes, there are some on Pine Street.

Greg: Oh, good. And is there a laundromat near here?

Mrs. Cook: Well, I think there's one across from the shopping center.

Greg: Thank you.

Mrs. Cook: By the way, there's a hair salon in the shopping center.

Greg: A hair salon?

3 GRAMMAR FOCUS

▶ *There is, there are; one, any, some*

Is there a laundromat near here?

    Yes, **there is**. There's **one** across from the shopping center.

    No, **there isn't**, but there's **one** next to the library.

Are there any grocery stores around here?

    Yes, **there are**. There are **some** nice stores on Pine Street.

    No, **there aren't**, but there are **some** on Third Avenue.

    No, **there aren't any** around here.

Prepositions
in
on
next to
near/close to
across from/opposite
in front of
in back of/behind
between
on the corner of

GRAMMAR PLUS *see page 139*

A Look at the map below. Write questions about these places.

| an ATM | coffee shops | a department store | an electronics store | Wi-Fi hot spots |
| gas stations | grocery stores | a gym | hotels | a post office |

Is there a gym around here?

Are there any restaurants on Main Street?

B PAIR WORK Ask and answer the questions you wrote in part A.

    A: Is there a gym around here?

    B: Yes, there is. There's one on Main Street next to the post office.

4 PRONUNCIATION Reduction of *there is/there are*

A Listen and practice. Notice how *there is* and *there are* are reduced in conversation, except for short answers.

Is there a bank near here?
Yes, **there is**. **There's** one on First Avenue.

Are there any coffee shops around here?
Yes, **there are**. **There are** some on Pine Street.

B Practice the questions and answers in Exercise 3, part B again.

5 SPEAKING A nice neighborhood

A PAIR WORK Choose a neighborhood in your city or town. Fill in the chart with information about the neighborhood. Write three examples for each category. Go to Exercises 1 and 3 for ideas and use your own ideas, too.

There is a/an . . . (where?)	There are some . . . (where?)
There isn't a/an . . . (where?)	There aren't any . . . (where?)

B GROUP WORK Take turns asking and answering questions with another pair about the neighborhoods. If you don't know about a place your new partners ask about, answer, "Sorry, I don't know." Who gets more "Yes" answers?

A: Is there a gym in your neighborhood?
B: Yes, there's one across from the park.
C: Are there any coffee shops?
D: No, there aren't any in our neighborhood.
B: Is there a bookstore in your neighborhood?
A: Sorry, I don't know.

6 LISTENING We need some directions.

A Listen to hotel guests ask about places to visit. Complete the chart.

Place	Location	Interesting? Yes	No
Flavors of Hollywood		☐	☐
Museum of Modern Art		☐	☐
City Zoo		☐	☐

B PAIR WORK Which place sounds the most interesting to you? Why?

7 SNAPSHOT

NEIGHBORHOODS

downtown/main street	the suburbs	a shopping district	a college campus
a business district	a theater district	an industrial district	a small town

What types of businesses are or aren't found in these neighborhoods?
Which areas do you visit often? Which areas do you hardly ever visit? Why?

8 CONVERSATION It's very convenient.

▶ Listen and practice.

 BARRY How do you like your new apartment, Alana?

 ALANA I love it. It's downtown, so it's very convenient.

 BARRY Downtown? Is there much traffic?

 ALANA Yeah, there's a lot. But I don't drive, so it's OK.

 BARRY Oh, that's right. Is there much crime in the area?

 ALANA No, it's pretty safe. The difference is the noise.

 BARRY Really? Is there a lot of noise?

 ALANA There's a lot on the weekend from the Italian restaurant downstairs.

 BARRY Oh, that's too bad. But is the food at the restaurant good?

 ALANA It's incredible! Hey, would you like to have dinner there on Saturday?

 BARRY Yes! I love Italian food.

9 GRAMMAR FOCUS

Quantifiers; *how many* and *how much*

Count nouns	Noncount nouns
Are there **many restaurants**?	Is there **much crime**?
Yes, there are **a lot**.	Yes, there's **a lot**.
There are **a few**.	There's **a little**.
No, there are**n't many**.	No, there is**n't much**.
No, there are**n't any**.	No, there is**n't any**.
No, there are **none**.	No, there's **none**.
How many restaurants are there?	**How much** crime is there?
There are 10 or 12.	There's a lot of crime.

GRAMMAR PLUS *see page 139*

A Write answers to these questions about your neighborhood.
Then practice with a partner.

1. Is there much parking?
2. Are there many apartment buildings?
3. How much traffic is there?
4. How many drugstores are there?
5. Is there much noise?
6. Are there many shopping malls?
7. Is there much pollution?
8. How many fast-food restaurants are there?

B GROUP WORK Write questions like those in part A
about these topics. Then ask and answer the questions.

cafés   crime   parks   trash   public transportation   schools   traffic lights

10 INTERCHANGE 8 Where are we?

Play a guessing game. Go to Interchange 8 on page 122.

11 WRITING My neighborhood

A Read this paragraph Kate wrote about her
neighborhood.

B Now write a paragraph about your
neighborhood. Describe what type of
neighborhood it is and what places are
or aren't in your area.

C PAIR WORK Read your partner's
paragraph. Ask follow-up questions
to get more information.

I live in a very nice neighborhood near my office, so I walk or ride my bike to work every morning. It's a very green area with many trees and a small but beautiful park. It's also very convenient. There is a shopping mall behind my building. In the mall, there are two drugstores, a bank, and a grocery store. And there is a café with great food and good prices. I get coffee there every morning. But there isn't a library, and most books at the bookstore are expensive. Oh well, nothing is perfect!

12 READING

A Scan the article. Check (✓) the neighborhood that is famous for nightlife.

☐ Roma Norte ☐ Shimokitazawa ☐ Pigneto

| Locations | Reservations | Shop | | Sign in | Register | 🔍 |

HIP NEIGHBORHOODS OF THE WORLD

Ⓐ Shimokitazawa, Tokyo

This is the place to be for fans of indie music! Head over to this creative neighborhood and discover record stores, concert halls, and theaters in the narrow streets. Shimokitazawa (or Shimokita, for short) is a relaxed place full of young people who visit the cafés and live music venues. Every year, there is a theater festival here. It's a very popular place for students.

Ⓑ Pigneto, Rome

La Sapienza, a famous college in Rome, is near this neighborhood. It's an extremely cool place to hang out. Pigneto has a huge choice of restaurants, cafés, and ice cream stores. Pigneto is famous for its nightlife. As you walk around, you hear electronic music coming from different clubs. People also come here for the Nuovo Cinema Aquila, the best place to see indie movies from around the world.

Ⓒ Roma Norte, Mexico City

This place is popular with artists, students, tourists, and musicians. Feeling hungry? Go to a huge food market, Mercado Roma, to taste delicious ceviche, squid torta, and other Mexican specialties. Next, check out the trendy restaurants for dinner, or shop for beautiful fashion items in the boutiques. There are hip T-shirts and sneakers for sale everywhere. There's locally made jewelry you can buy, too!

B Read the article. Then write the letter of the paragraph where these things are mentioned.

1. _____ local jewelry
2. _____ festivals
3. _____ indie movies
4. _____ record stores
5. _____ food specialties
6. _____ a college
7. _____ theaters
8. _____ ice cream

C PAIR WORK What's your favorite neighborhood in your city or country? What is interesting about it? What do you like to do there?

How's the neighborhood? **55**

Units 7–8 Progress check

SELF-ASSESSMENT

How well can you do these things? Check (✓) the boxes.

I can . . .	Very well	OK	A little
Understand descriptions of past events (Ex. 1)	☐	☐	☐
Describe events in the past (Ex. 1)	☐	☐	☐
Ask and answer questions about past activities (Ex. 2)	☐	☐	☐
Give and understand simple directions (Ex. 3)	☐	☐	☐
Talk about my neighborhood (Ex. 4)	☐	☐	☐

1 LISTENING Jimmy's weekend

▶ **A** A thief robbed a house on Saturday. A detective is questioning Jimmy. The pictures show what Jimmy really did on Saturday. Listen to their conversation. Are Jimmy's answers true (**T**) or false (**F**)?

1:00 P.M. T F 3:00 P.M. T F 5:00 P.M. T F 6:00 P.M. T F 8:00 P.M. T F 10:30 P.M. T F

B PAIR WORK What did Jimmy really do? Use the pictures to retell the story.

2 DISCUSSION How good is your memory?

A Do you remember what you did yesterday? Check (✓) the things you did. Then add two other things you did.

☐ got up early ☐ went to class ☐ did the laundry ☐ went to bed late
☐ exercised ☐ ate at a restaurant ☐ did the dishes ☐ _____
☐ texted a friend ☐ went shopping ☐ went online ☐ _____

B GROUP WORK Ask questions about each thing in part A.

A: Did you get up early yesterday?
B: No, I didn't. I got up at 10:00. I was very tired.

3 SPEAKING What's your neighborhood like?

A Create a neighborhood. Add five places to "My map." Choose from this list. Add plural words two or more times.

a bank   a bookstore   cafés   drugstores   gas stations   a gym   a theater

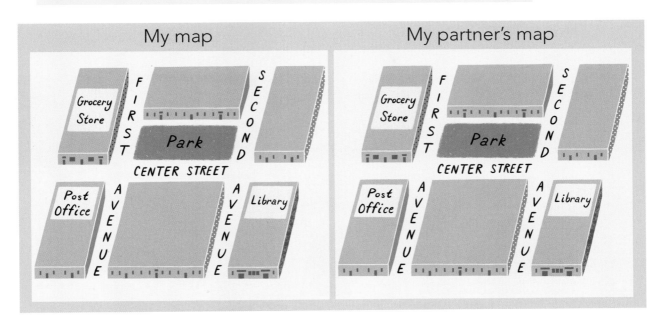

B **PAIR WORK** Ask questions about your partner's map. (But don't look!) Draw the places on "My partner's map." Then compare your maps.

A: Are there any gas stations in the neighborhood?

B: Yes, there are two. There's one on the corner of Center Street and First Avenue and one on Center Street across from the park.

4 ROLE PLAY Tell me about your neighborhood.

Student A: Imagine you are a visitor in Student B's neighborhood. Ask questions about it.

Student B: Imagine a visitor wants to find out about your neighborhood. Answer the visitor's questions.

A: Is there much crime?

B: There isn't much. It's a very safe neighborhood.

A: Is there much noise?

B: Well, yes, it's a shopping district, so . . .

Change roles and try the role play again.

topics to ask about
buildings
crime
noise
parking
parks
places to shop
pollution
public transportation
schools
traffic

WHAT'S NEXT?

Look at your Self-assessment again. Do you need to review anything?

Interchange activities

A CLASS ACTIVITY Add one more question to the chart. Go around the class and interview three classmates. Complete the chart.

	Classmate 1	Classmate 2	Classmate 3
What's your first name?			
What's your last name?			
What city are you from?			
When's your birthday?			
What's your favorite color?			
What are your hobbies?			

B GROUP WORK Compare your information. Then discuss these questions.

Who . . . ?

has a long first name   has the next birthday

has a long last name   likes orange or brown

is not from a big city   has an interesting hobby

A CLASS ACTIVITY Add one more question to the chart. Answer these questions about yourself. Then interview two classmates. Write their names and the times they do each thing.

What time do you . . . ?	Me	Name _____	Name _____
get up during the week			
get up on weekends			
have breakfast			
leave for school or work			
get home during the week			
have dinner			
go to bed during the week			
_____			

B PAIR WORK Whose schedule is similar to yours? Tell your partner.

A: Amir and I have similar schedules. We both get up at 7:00 and have breakfast at 7:30.

B: I leave for work at 7:30, but Nikki leaves for school at . . .

useful expressions

We both . . . at . . .

We . . . at different times.

My schedule is different from my two classmates' schedules.

STUDENT A

A You want to sell these things. Write your "asking price" for each item.

TABLET

asking price: _____

sold for: _____

HEADPHONES

asking price: _____

sold for: _____

ARMCHAIR

asking price: _____

sold for: _____

SKATEBOARD

asking price: _____

sold for: _____

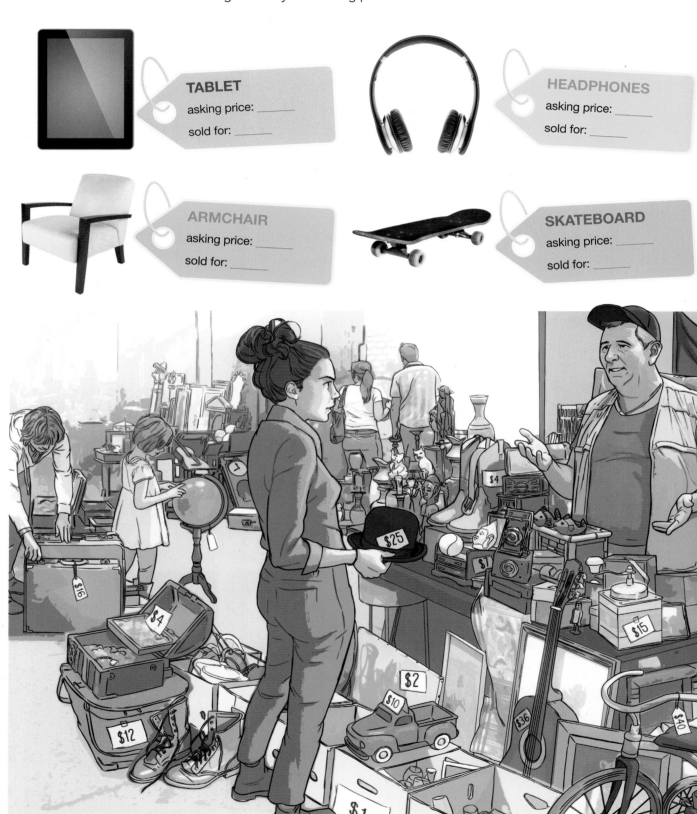

STUDENT B

A You want to sell these things. Write your "asking price" for each item.

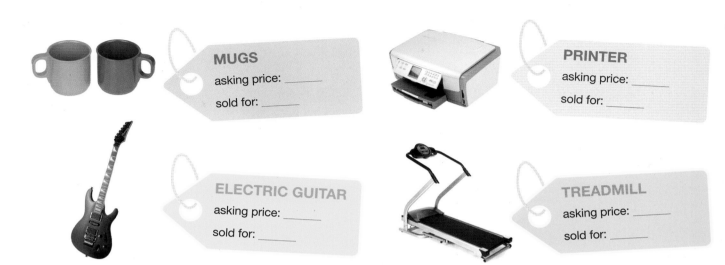

MUGS
asking price: _____
sold for: _____

PRINTER
asking price: _____
sold for: _____

ELECTRIC GUITAR
asking price: _____
sold for: _____

TREADMILL
asking price: _____
sold for: _____

STUDENTS A AND B

B PAIR WORK Now choose three things you want to buy. Get the best price for each one. Then write what each item "sold for" on the price tag.

A: How much is the tablet computer?
B: It's only $70.
A: Wow! That's expensive!
B: Well, how about $35?
A: No. That's still too much. I'll give you $30 for it.
B: Sold! It's yours.

C GROUP WORK Compare your earnings in groups. Who made the most money at the flea market?

go bike riding

go to a street fair

go dancing

do the laundry

clean the house

A Write three things you need to do and three things you want to do this weekend. Include the days of the week and the times.

I need to . . .	I want to . . .

B **PAIR WORK** Invite your partner to do things on the weekend. Accept or decline invitations. If you decline an invitation, explain why. Agree on two activities to do together.

A: Would you like to see a movie on Saturday at 8:00 P.M.?

B: I'd like to, but I need to study for a test. Would you like to go to the park on Sunday at 10:00 A.M.?

A: Yes, I would. And would you like to . . . ?

C **GROUP WORK** Get together with another pair. Can you agree on two things to do together?

D **CLASS WORK** Explain your group's choices to the class.
"Eu-jin wanted to go to the park on Sunday at 10 A.M., but Serhat needs to visit his aunt on Sunday morning, so we're going out for lunch on Sunday at . . ."

CLASS ACTIVITY Go around the class telling your classmates three activities that members of your family are doing these days. Two activities have to be true, but one needs to be false! Can your classmates guess which activity is false with only two questions?

learning a foreign language

raising a child

renovating the house

working in another country

writing a blog

your ideas

learning to drive

going to college

traveling around the world

playing in a band

playing on a team

A: My brother is working in Berlin and his wife is studying German there. My niece is learning three languages at school: German, English, and Spanish.

B: Is your brother really working in Berlin?

A: Yes, he is.

B: Is your niece really learning Spanish?

A: No, she's not! She's learning German and English, but she isn't learning Spanish.

A CLASS ACTIVITY Add two items to the chart. Does anyone in your class do these things? How often and how well? Go around the class and find one person for each activity.

	Name	How often?	How well?
bake cookies			
cook			
cut hair			
do card tricks			
fix things			
play an instrument			
sing			
do yoga			

A: Do you bake cookies?
B: Yes, I do.
A: How often do you bake cookies?
B: Once a month.
A: Really? And how well do you bake?

B GROUP WORK Imagine there's a fundraiser to buy new books for the school library this weekend. Who do you think can help? Choose three people from your class. Explain your choices.

A: Let's ask Lydia to help with the fundraiser.
B: Why Lydia?
A: Because she bakes cookies very well.
C: Yes, she really does. And Mariana is very good at fixing things. Let's ask her, too!

GROUP WORK Play the board game. Follow these instructions.

1. Write your initials on small pieces of paper. These are your game pieces.

2. Take turns by tossing a coin: If the coin lands face up, move two spaces.
If the coin lands face down, move one space.

3. When you land on a space, answer the question. Answer any follow-up questions.

4. If you land on "Free question," another player asks you any question.

A: I'll go first. OK, one space. Last night, I met my best friend.

B: Oh, yeah? Where did you go?

A: We went to the movies.

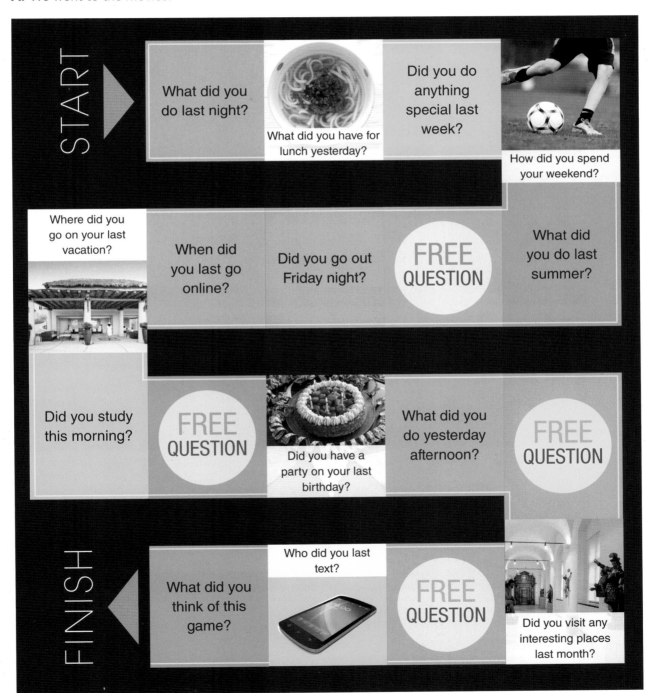

CLASS ACTIVITY Play a guessing game. Follow these instructions.

1. Get into two teams, A and B.
2. Each team chooses one of the locations below. Keep it a secret!
3. Each team chooses a teammate to guess the other team's location. He or she is the guesser.
4. Show your location to all the students on the other team, except their guesser.
5. Take turns giving your guessers one clue at a time until they guess the location. Use *There is/ There are* plus a quantifier. You cannot give more than 10 clues. Your team can get 1 to 10 points, depending on how many clues you need to give your guesser (1 clue = 1 point) before he or she guesses the right location. Remember: you don't want to get many points!
6. At the end of the game, the team with fewer points wins.

an airport	a bank	a bookstore	a café
a clothing store	a drugstore	a grocery store	a gym
a hair salon	a hospital	a movie theater	a newstand
an outdoor market	a park	a shopping mall	a stadium

A: There is a lot of food here. Where are we?
B: You're in a grocery store.
C: No. There aren't any walls here. This isn't a building.
B: You're at an outdoor market!
A: Correct! We're at an outdoor market.

This page is intentionally left blank

Grammar plus

1 Statements with *be*; possessive adjectives page 3

> ■ Don't confuse contractions of *be* with possessive adjectives: **You're** a student. **Your** class is English 1. (NOT: ~~You're class is English 1.~~) **He's** my classmate. **His** name is Ricardo. (NOT: ~~He's name is Ricardo.~~)

Choose the correct words.

1. This **is** / **are** Dulce Castelo. **She's** / **Her** a new student from Santo Domingo.
2. My name **am** / **is** Sergio. **I'm** / **He's** from Brazil.
3. My brother and I **is** / **are** students here. **Our** / **We're** names are Nate and Chad.
4. **He's** / **His** Kento. **He's** / **His** 19 years old.
5. **They're** / **Their** in my English class. **It's** / **Its** a big class.

2 Wh-questions with *be* page 4

> ■ Use *What* to ask about things: **What's** in your bag? Use *Where* to ask about places: **Where's** your friend from? Use *Who* to ask about people: **Who's** your teacher? Use *What . . . like?* to ask for a description: **What's** your friend **like**?

Match the questions with the answers.

1. Who's that? ___f___
2. Where's your teacher? _____
3. What are your friends like? _____
4. Where's she from? _____
5. Who are they? _____
6. What's his name? _____

   a. They're really nice.
   b. She's from South Korea.
   c. They're my brother and sister.
   d. His name is Daniel.
   e. He's in class.
   f. That's our new classmate.

3 Yes/No questions and short answers with *be* page 5

> ■ Use short answers to answer yes/no questions. Don't use contractions with short answers with Yes: **Are you** from Mexico? Yes, **I am**. (NOT: ~~Yes, I'm.~~)

Complete the conversations.

1. **A:** ___Are they___ in your class?
   B: No, _____. They're in English 2.
2. **A:** Hi! _____ in this class?
   B: Yes, _____. I'm a new student here.
3. **A:** _____ from the United States?
   B: No, _____. We're from Calgary, Canada.
4. **A:** Hi, Monica. _____ free?
   B: No, _____. I'm on my way to class.
5. **A:** That's the new student. _____ from Paraguay?
   B: No, _____. He's from Uruguay.
6. **A:** _____ from Indonesia?
   B: Yes, _____. She's from Jakarta.

1 Simple present Wh-questions and statements page 10

Statements

- Verbs with *he/she/it* end in –*s*: He/She **walks** to school. BUT I/You/We/They **walk** to school.

- *Have*, *go*, and *do* are irregular with *he/she/it*: She **has** a class at 1:00. He **goes** to school at night. She **does** her homework before school.

Wh-questions

- Use *does* in questions with *he/she/it* and *do* with all the others: Where does he/she/it live? Where do I/you/we/they live?

- Don't add –*s* to the verb: Where does she **live**? (NOT: Where does she lives?)

Complete the conversations with the correct form of the verbs in parentheses.

1. A: I _____have_____ (have) good news! Mona _____ (have) a new job.
   B: How _____ she _____ (like) it?
   A: She _____ (love) it. The hours are great.
   B: What time _____ she _____ (start)?
   A: She _____ (start) at ten and _____ (finish) at four.

2. A: What _____ you _____ (do)?
   B: I'm a teacher.
   A: What _____ you _____ (teach)?
   B: I _____ (teach) Spanish and English.
   A: Really? My sister _____ (teach) English, too.

2 Time expressions page 12

- Use *in* with *the morning/afternoon/evening*. Use *at* with *night*: He goes to school **in** the afternoon and works **at** night. BUT: **on** Friday night.

- Use *at* with clock times: She gets up **at** 7:00.

- Use *on* with days: He gets up early **on** weekdays. She has class **on** Mondays.

Complete the conversation with time expressions from the box.
You can use some words more than once.

at	early	in	on	until

A: How's your new job?

B: I love it, but the hours are difficult. I start work _____ 6:30 A.M., and I work _____ 3:30.

A: That's interesting! I work the same hours, but I work _____ night. I start _____ 6:30 _____ the evening and finish _____ 3:30 _____ the morning.

B: Wow! What time do you get up?

A: Well, I get home _____ 4:30 and go to bed _____ 5:30. And I sleep _____ 2:00. But I only work _____ weekends, so it's OK. What about you?

B: Oh, I work _____ Monday, Wednesday, and Friday. And I get up _____ – around 5:00 A.M.

1 Demonstratives; *one, ones* `page 17`

- With singular nouns, use *this* for a thing that is nearby and *that* for a thing that is not nearby: How much is **this** hat here? How much is **that** hat over there?

- With plural nouns, use *these* for things that are nearby and *those* for things that are not nearby: How much are **these** earrings here? How much are **those** earrings over there?

- Use *one* to replace a singular noun: I like the red hat. I like the red **one**. Use *ones* to replace plural nouns: I like the green bags. I like the green **ones**.

Choose the correct words.

1. **A:** Excuse me. How much are **this** / (**these**) shoes?
   B: **It's** / **They're** $279.
   A: And how much is **this** / **that** bag over there?
   B: **It's** / **They're** only $129.
   A: And are the two gray **one** / **ones** $129, too?
   B: No. **That** / **Those** are only $119.
   A: Oh! **This** / **That** store is really expensive.

2. **A:** Can I help you?
   B: Yes, please. I really like **these** / **those** jeans over there. How much **is it** / **are they**?
   A: Which **one** / **ones**? Do you mean **this** / **these**?
   B: No, the black **one** / **ones**.
   A: Let me look. Oh, **it's** / **they're** $35.99.
   B: That's not bad. And how much is **this** / **that** sweater here?
   A: **It's** / **They're** only $9.99.

2 Preferences; comparisons with adjectives `page 20`

- For adjectives with one syllable or adjectives of two syllables ending in –y, add –er to form the comparative:
  cheap → cheaper; nice → nicer; big → bigger, pretty → prettier.

- For adjectives with two syllables not ending in –y or adjectives of three or more syllables, use *more* + adjective to form the comparative: stylish → more stylish, expensive → more expensive.

A Write the comparatives of these adjectives.

1. attractive   _more attractive_
2. happy   _____
3. exciting   _____
4. friendly   _____

5. interesting   _____
6. reasonable   _____
7. sad   _____
8. warm   _____

B Answer the questions. Use the first word in the parentheses in your answer.
Then write another sentence with the second word.

1. Which pants do you prefer, the cotton ones or the wool ones? (wool / attractive)
   I prefer the wool ones. They're more attractive than the cotton ones.

2. Which ring do you like better, the gold one or the silver one? (silver / interesting)
   _____

3. Which one do you prefer, the silk blouse or the cotton blouse? (silk / pretty)
   _____

4. Which ones do you like more, the black shoes or the purple ones? (purple / cheap)
   _____

UNIT 4

1 Simple present questions; short answers [page 23]

- Use *do* + base form for yes/no questions and short answers with *I/you/we/they*: **Do** I/you/we/they **like** rock? Yes, I/you/we/they **do**. No, I/you/we/they **don't.**
- Use *does* in yes/no questions and short answers with *he/she/it*: **Does** he/she **like** rock? Yes, he/she **does**. No, he/she **doesn't.**
- Use *don't* and *doesn't* + base form for negative statements: I **don't** like horror movies. He **doesn't like** action movies.
- Remember: Don't add –s to the base form: Does she **like** rock? (NOT: ~~Does she likes rock?~~)
- Subject pronouns (*I, you, he, she, it, we, they*) usually come before a verb. Object pronouns (*me, you, him, her, it, us, them*) usually come after a verb: He likes **her**, but she doesn't like **him**.

A Complete the questions and short answers.

1. A: _Do you play_ (play) a musical instrument?
   B: Yes, _I do_____. I play the guitar.
2. A: _____ (like) Carrie Underwood?
   B: No, _____. John doesn't like country music.
3. A: _____ (like) talk shows?
   B: Yes, _____. Lisa is a big fan of them.
4. A: _____ (watch) the news on TV?
   B: Yes, _____. Kevin and I watch the news every night.
5. A: _____ (like) hip-hop?
   B: No, _____. But I love R&B.
6. A: _____ (listen to) jazz?
   B: No, _____. But my parents listen to a lot of classical music.

B Complete the sentences with object pronouns.

1. We don't listen to hip-hop because we really don't like __it__.
2. We love your voice. Please sing for _____.
3. These sunglasses are great. Do you like _____?
4. Who is that man? Do you know _____?
5. Beth looks great in green. It's a really good color for _____.

2 *Would*; verb + *to* + verb [page 26]

- Don't use a contraction in affirmative short answers with *would*: **Would** you **like to go to** the game? Yes, I **would**. (NOT: ~~Yes, I'd.~~)

Unscramble the questions and answers to complete the conversation.

A: tonight   to see   would you like   with me   a movie
_____?
B: I would.   yes,   what   to see   would you like
_____?
A: the new Matt Damon movie   to see   I'd like
_____.
B: OK. That's a great idea!

UNIT 5

1 Present continuous page 32

■ Use the present continuous to talk about actions that are happening now: What **are** you **doing (these days)**? I'**m studying** English.

■ The present continuous is present of *be* + *–ing*. For verbs ending in *e*, drop the *e* and add *–ing*: have → having, live → living.

■ For verbs ending in vowel + consonant, double the consonant and add *–ing*: sit → sitting.

Write questions with the words in parentheses and the present continuous. Then complete the responses with short answers or the verbs in the box.

| live   study   take   ✓ teach   work |

1. **A:** (what / your sister / do / these days) <u>What's your sister doing these days?</u>
   B: <u>She's teaching</u> English.
   A: Really? (she / live / abroad) _____
   B: Yes, _____. She _____ in South Korea.
2. **A:** (how / you / spend / your summer) _____
   B: I _____ part-time. I _____ two classes also.
   A: (what / you / take) _____
   B: My friend and I _____ photography and Japanese. We like our classes a lot.

2 Quantifiers page 34

■ Use *a lot of, all, few, nearly all* before plural nouns: **A lot of/All/Few/Nearly all** families are small. Use *no one* before a verb: **No one** gets married before the age of 18.

■ *Nearly all* means "almost all."

Read the sentences about the small town of Monroe. Rewrite the sentences using the quantifiers in the box. Use each quantifier only once.

| a lot of   all   few   nearly all   ✓ no one |

1. In Monroe, 0% of the people drive before the age of 16.
   <u>In Monroe, no one drives before the age of 16.</u>
2. Ninety-eight percent of students finish high school.
   _____
3. One hundred percent of children start school by the age of six.
   _____
4. Eighty-nine percent of couples have more than one child.
   _____
5. Five percent of families have more than four children.
   _____

UNIT 6

1 Adverbs of frequency page 37

- Adverbs of frequency (*always, almost always, usually, often, sometimes, hardly ever, almost never, never*) usually come before the main verb: She **never plays** tennis. I **almost always eat** breakfast. BUT Adverbs of frequency usually come after the verb *be*: I**'m always** late.
- *Usually* and *sometimes* can begin a sentence: **Usually** I walk to work. **Sometimes** I exercise in the morning.
- Some frequency expressions usually come at the end of a sentence: *every day, once a week, twice a month, three times a year:* Do you exercise **every day**? I exercise **three times a week**.

Put the words in order to make questions. Then complete the answers with the words in parentheses.

1. you   what   weekends   usually   do   do   on
   Q: _What do you usually do on weekends?_
   A: I _____ (often / play sports)

2. ever   you   go jogging   do   with a friend
   Q: _____
   A: No, _____ (always / alone)

3. you   play   do   basketball   how often
   Q: _____
   A: I _____ (four times a week)

4. do you   what   in the evening   usually   do
   Q: _____
   A: My family and I _____ (almost always / go online)

5. go   how often   you   do   to the gym
   Q: _____
   A: I _____ (never)

2 Questions with *how*; short answers page 40

- Don't confuse *good* and *well*. Use the adjective *good* with *be* and the adverb *well* with other verbs: How **good** are you at soccer? BUT How **well** do you play soccer?

Complete the questions with *How* and a word from the box.
Then match the questions and the answers.

good   long   often   well

1. _____ do you lift weights? _____   a. Not very well, but I love it.
2. _____ do you play basketball? _____   b. About six hours a week.
3. _____ are you at volleyball? _____   c. Not very often. I prefer martial arts.
4. _____ do you spend at the gym? _____   d. Pretty good, but I hate it.

1 Simple past   page 45

■ Use *did* with the base form – not the past form – of the main verb in questions: How **did** you **spend** the weekend? (NOT: ~~How did you spent . . .?~~)

■ Use *didn't* with the base form in negative statements: We **didn't go** shopping. (NOT: ~~We didn't went shopping.~~)

Complete the conversation.

A: _____Did_____ you _____have_____ (have) a good weekend?

B: Yes, I _____. I _____ (have) a great time. My sister and I _____ (go) shopping on Saturday. We _____ (spend) all day at the mall.

A: _____ you _____ (buy) anything special?

B: I _____ (buy) a new laptop. And I _____ (get) some new clothes, too.

A: Lucky you! What clothes _____ you _____ (buy)?

B: Well, I _____ (need) some new boots. I _____ (get) some great ones at Great Times Department Store. What about you? What _____ you _____ (do) on Saturday?

A: I _____ (not, do) anything special. I _____ (stay) home and _____ (work) around the house. Oh, but I _____ (see) a really good movie on TV. And then I _____ (make) dinner with my mother. I actually _____ (enjoy) the day.

2 Past of *be*   page 47

■ Present		Past
am/is	→	**was**
are	→	**were**

Rewrite the sentences. Find another way to write each sentence using *was*, *wasn't*, *were*, or *weren't* and the words in parentheses.

1. Bruno didn't come to class yesterday. (in class)
   Bruno wasn't in class yesterday.

2. He worked all day. (at work)
   _____

3. Bruno and his co-workers worked on Saturday, too. (at work)
   _____

4. They didn't go to work on Sunday. (at work)
   _____

5. Did Bruno stay home on Sunday? (at home)
   _____

6. Where did Bruno go on Sunday? (on Sunday)
   _____

7. He and his brother went to a baseball game. (at a baseball game)
   _____

8. They stayed at the park until 7:00. (at the park)
   _____

UNIT 8

1 There is, there are; one, any, some ⟋ page 51

- Don't use a contraction in a short answer with *Yes*: Is there a hotel near here? Yes, **there is**. (NOT: ~~Yes, there's.~~)
- Use *some* in affirmative statements and *any* in negative statements: There are **some** grocery stores in my neighborhood, but there aren't **any** restaurants. Use *any* in most questions: Are there **any** nice stores around here?

Complete the conversations. Choose the correct words.

1. **A:** **Is** / **Are** there any supermarkets in this neighborhood?
   B: No, there **isn't** / **aren't**, but there are **one** / **some** on Main Street.
   A: And **is** / **are** there a post office near here?
   B: Yes, **there's** / **there is**. It's across from the bank.

2. **A:** **Is** / **Are** there a gas station around here?
   B: Yes, **there's** / **there are** one behind the shopping center.
   A: Great! And are there **a** / **any** coffee shops nearby?
   B: Yes, there's a good **one** / **some** in the shopping center.

2 Quantifiers; *how many* and *how much* ⟋ page 54

- Use *a lot* with both count and noncount nouns: Are there many traffic lights on First Avenue? Yes, there are **a lot**. Is there much traffic? Yes, there's **a lot**.
- Use *any* – not *none* – in negative statements: How much traffic is there on your street? There **isn't any**. = There**'s none**. (NOT: ~~There isn't none.~~)
- Use *How many* with count nouns: **How many books** do you have?
- Use *How much* with noncount nouns: **How much traffic** is there?

A Complete the conversations. Choose the correct words.

1. **A:** Is there **many** / **much** traffic in your city?
   B: Well, there's **a few** / **a little**.

2. **A:** Are there **many** / **much** Wi-Fi hotspots around here?
   B: No, there aren't **many** / **none**.

3. **A:** **How many** / **How much** restaurants are there in your neighborhood?
   B: There **is** / **are** a lot.

4. **A:** **How many** / **How much** noise **is** / **are** there in your city?
   B: There's **much** / **none**. It's very quiet.

B Write questions with the words in parentheses. Use *much* or *many*.

1. **A:** <u>Is there much pollution in your neighborhood?</u> (pollution)
   B: No, there isn't. My neighborhood is very clean.

2. **A:** _____ (parks)
   B: Yes, there are. They're great for families.

3. **A:** _____ (crime)
   B: There's none. It's a very safe part of the city.

4. **A:** _____ (laundromats)
   B: There aren't any. A lot of people have their own washing machines.

Grammar plus answer key

Unit 1

1 **Statements with *be*; possessive adjectives**
1. This **is** Dulce Castelo. **She's** a new student from Santo Domingo.
2. My name **is** Sergio. **I'm** from Brazil.
3. My brother and I **are** students here. **Our** names are Nate and Chad.
4. **He's** Kento. **He's** 19 years old.
5. **They're** in my English class. **It's** a big class.

2 **Wh-questions with *be***
2. e   3. a   4. b   5. c   6. d

3 **Yes/No questions and short answers with *be***
1. A: **Are** they in your class?
   B: No, **they're not / they aren't**. They're in English 2.
2. A: Hi! **Are you** in this class?
   B: Yes, **I am**. I'm a new student here.
3. A: **Are you** from the United States?
   B: No, **we're not / we aren't**. We're from Calgary, Canada.
4. A: Hi, Monica. **Are you** free?
   B: No, **I'm not**. I'm on my way to class.
5. A: That's the new student. **Is he** from Paraguay?
   B: No, **he's not / he isn't**. He's from Uruguay.
6. A: **Is she** from Indonesia?
   B: Yes, **she is**. She's from Jakarta.

Unit 2

1 **Simple present Wh-questions and statements**
1. A: I **have** good news! Mona **has** a new job.
   B: How **does** she **like** it?
   A: She **loves** it. The hours are great.
   B: What time **does** she **start**?
   A: She **starts** at ten and **finishes** at four.
2. A: What **do** you **do**?
   B: I'm a teacher.
   A: What **do** you **teach**?
   B: I **teach** Spanish and English.
   A: Really? My sister **teaches** English, too.

2 **Time expressions**
B: I love it, but the hours are difficult. I start work **at** 6:30 A.M., and I work **until** 3:30.
A: That's interesting! I work the same hours, but I work **at** night. I start **at** 6:30 **in** the evening and finish **at** 3:30 **in** the morning.
B: Wow! What time do you get up?
A: Well, I get home **at** 4:30 and go to bed **at** 5:30. And I sleep **until** 2:00. But I only work **on** weekends, so it's OK. What about you?
B: Oh, I work **on** Monday, Wednesday, and Friday. And I get up **early** – around 5:00 A.M.

Unit 3

1 **Demonstratives; *one, ones***
1. A: Excuse me. How much are **these** shoes?
   B: **They're** $279.
   A: And how much is **that** bag over there?
   B: **It's** only $129.
   A: And are the two gray **ones** $129, too?
   B: No. **Those** are only $119.
   A: Oh! **This** store is really expensive.
2. A: Can I help you?
   B: Yes, please. I really like **those** jeans over there. How much **are they**?
   A: Which **ones**? Do you mean **these**?
   B: No, the black **ones**.
   A: Let me look. Oh, **they're** $35.99.
   B: That's not bad. And how much is **this** sweater here?
   A: **It's** only $9.99.

2 **Preferences; comparisons with adjectives**
A
2. happier
3. more exciting
4. friendlier
5. more interesting
6. more reasonable
7. sadder
8. warmer
B
2. I like the silver one (better). It's more interesting.
3. I prefer the silk one. It's prettier.
4. I like the purple ones (more). They're cheaper.

Unit 4

1 **Simple present questions; short answers**
A
2. A: **Does John like** Carrie Underwood?
   B: No, **he doesn't**. John doesn't like country music.
3. A: **Does Lisa like** talk shows?
   B: Yes, **she does**. Lisa is a big fan of them.
4. A: **Do you / you and Kevin watch** the news on TV?
   B: Yes, **we do**. Kevin and I watch the news every night.
5. A: **Do you like** hip-hop?
   B: No, **I don't**. But I love R&B.
6. A: **Do your parents listen to** jazz?
   B: No, **they don't**. But my parents listen to a lot of classical music.
B
2. us   3. them   4. him   5. her

2 ***Would*; verb + *to* + verb**
A: Would you like to see a movie with me tonight?
B: Yes, I would. What would you like to see?
A: I'd like to see the new Matt Damon movie.

Unit 5

1 Present continuous

1. A: Really? **Is she living abroad?**
   B: Yes, **she is**. She**'s living / is living** in South Korea.
2. A: **How are you spending your summer?**
   B: **I'm working** part-time. **I'm taking** two classes also.
   A: **What are you taking?**
   B: My friend and I **are studying** photography and Japanese. We like our classes a lot.

2 Quantifiers

2. Nearly all students finish high school.
3. All children start school by the age of six.
4. A lot of couples have more than one child.
5. Few families have more than four children.

Unit 6

1 Adverbs of frequency

1. A: **I often play sports.**
2. Q: **Do you ever go jogging with a friend?**
   A: No, **I always jog / go jogging alone.**
3. Q: **How often do you play basketball?**
   A: **I play (basketball) four times a week.**
4. Q: **What do you usually do in the evening?**
   A: My family and I **almost always go online.**
5. Q: **How often do you go to the gym?**
   A: **I never go (to the gym).**

2 Questions with *how*; short answers

1. **How often** do you lift weights? c
2. **How well** do you play basketball? a
3. **How good** are you at volleyball? d
4. **How long** do you spend at the gym? b

Unit 7

1 Simple past

B: Yes, I **did**. I **had** a great time. My sister and I **went** shopping on Saturday. We **spent** all day at the mall.
A: **Did** you **buy** anything special?
B: I **bought** a new laptop. And I **got** some new clothes, too.
A: Lucky you! What clothes **did** you **buy**?
B: Well, I **needed** some new boots. I **got** some great ones at Great Times Department Store. What about you? What **did** you **do** on Saturday?
A: I **didn't do** anything special. I **stayed** home and **worked** around the house. Oh, but I **saw** a really good movie on TV. And then I **made** dinner with my mother. I actually **enjoyed** the day.

2 Past of *be*

2. He was at work all day.
3. Bruno and his co-workers were at work on Saturday, too.
4. They weren't at work on Sunday.
5. Was Bruno at home on Sunday?
6. Where was Bruno on Sunday?
7. He and his brother were at a baseball game.
8. They were at the park until 7:00.

Unit 8

1 There is, there are; one, any, some

1. A: **Are** there any supermarkets in this neighborhood?
   B: No, there **aren't**, but there are **some** on Main Street.
   A: And **is** there a post office near here?
   B: Yes, **there is**. It's across from the bank.
2. A: **Is** there a gas station around here?
   B: Yes, **there's** one behind the shopping center.
   A: Great! And are there **any** coffee shops nearby?
   B: Yes, there's a good **one** in the shopping center.

2 Quantifiers; *how many* and *how much*

A

1. A: Is there **much** traffic in your city?
   B: Well, there's a **little**.
2. A: Are there **many** Wi-Fi hotspots around here?
   B: No, there aren't **many**.
3. A: **How many** restaurants are there in your neighborhood?
   B: There **are** a lot.
4. A: **How much** noise **is** there in your city?
   B: There's **none**. It's very quiet

B

2. A: Are there many parks (in your neighborhood)?
3. A: Is there much crime (in your neighborhood)?
4. A: Are there many laundromats (in your neighborhood)?

Credits

The authors and publishers acknowledge the following sources of copyright material and are grateful for the permissions granted. While every effort has been made, it has not always been possible to identify the sources of all the material used, or to trace all copyright holders. If any omissions are brought to our notice, we will be happy to include the appropriate acknowledgements on reprinting and in the next update to the digital edition, as applicable.

Keys: E = Exercise; T = Top, B = Below, TR = Top Right, TL = Top Left, BR = Below Right, BL = Below Left, C = Centre, CR = Centre Right, CL = Centre Left, L = Left, R = Right, BC = Below Centre, B/G = Background.

Illustrations

337 Jon (KJA Artists): 17(T); **Mark Duffin**: 17(B), 80; **Thomas Girard** (Good Illustration): 50, 64, 66, 78(B), 108, 116–117; **Daniel Gray-Barnett**: 51, 57, 92; **Quino Marin** (The Organisation): 17(C), 18, 56, 70, 120; **Gavin Reece** (New Division): 2, 3, 5, 61, 123, 124; **Paul Williams** (Sylvie Poggio Artists): 60, 78(T).

Photos

Back cover (woman with whiteboard): Jenny Acheson/Stockbyte/GettyImages; Back cover (whiteboard): Nemida/GettyImages; Back cover (man using phone): Betsie Van Der Meer/Taxi/GettyImages; Back cover (woman smiling): PeopleImages.com/DigitalVision/GettyImages; Back cover (name tag): Tetra Images/GettyImages; Back cover (handshake): David Lees/Taxi/GettyImages; p. v: Caiaimage/Chris Ryan/GettyImages; p. 2 (header), p. vi (Unit 1): M G Therin Weise/Photographer's Choice RF/GettyImages; p. 4 (photo 1): Hill Street Studios/Tobin Rogers/Blend Images/GettyImages; p. 4 (photo 2): Steve Debenport/E+/GettyImages; p. 4 (photo 3): Monty Rakusen/Cultura/GettyImages; p. 4 (photo 4): Jose Luis Pelaez Inc/Blend Images/GettyImages; p. 4 (photo 5): Peter Cade/Iconica/GettyImages; p. 4 (photo 6): Sofia Bagdasarian/EyeEm/GettyImages; p. 4 (photo 7): Jon Feingersh/Blend Images/GettyImages; p. 4 (photo 8): Echo/Cultura/GettyImages; p. 6 (T): Caiaimage/Sam Edwards/Caiaimage/GettyImages; p. 6 (B): DragonImages/iStock/Getty Images Plus/GettyImages; p. 7 (T): Jamie McCarthy/Getty Images Entertainment/GettyImages; p. 7 (B): Pool/Samir Hussein/WireImage/GettyImages; p. 8 (header), p. vi (Unit 2): Hero Images/GettyImages; p. 8 (babysitter): Jonas unruh/E+/GettyImages; p. 8 (fitness instructor): Jutta Klee/Canopy/GettyImages; p. 8 (office assistant): Sturti/E+/GettyImages; p. 8 (sales associate): Matthias Tunger/DigitalVision/GettyImages; p. 8 (social media assistant): Tim Robberts/Taxi/GettyImages; p. 8 (tutor): Prasit photo/Moment/GettyImages; p. 9 (T): Hero Images/GettyImages; p. 9 (C): Westend61/GettyImages; p. 9 (B): Westend61/GettyImages; p. 10: Steve Debenport/E+/GettyImages; p. 11 (T): Marc Romanelli/Blend Images/GettyImages; p. 11 (B): Yellow Dog Productions/Iconica/GettyImages; p. 11 (taxi driver): Monty Rakusen/Cultura/GettyImages; p. 11 (Kristina): Yellow Dog Productions/Iconica/GettyImages; p. 13 (Danny): tulpahn/iStock/Getty Images Plus/GettyImages; p. 13 (Carla): Image Source/DigitalVision/GettyImages; p. 13 (Nico): Golero/E+/GettyImages; p. 13 (Lisa): Portishead1/E+/GettyImages; p. 14: Fabrice LEROUGE/ONOKY/GettyImages; p. 15 (engineer): B Busco/Photographer's Choice/GettyImages; p. 15 (caregiver): Maskot/GettyImages; p. 15 (electrician): Pamela Moore/E+/GettyImages; p. 15 (IT worker): Echo/Cultura/GettyImages; p. 15 (B): i love images/Cultura/GettyImages; p. 16 (header), p. vi (Unit 3): John Fedele/Blend Images/GettyImages; p. 16 (white mug): Steve Gorton/Dorling Kindersley/GettyImages; p. 16 (blue mug): Dorling Kindersley/GettyImages; p. 16 (green mug): Denis Gladkiy/iStock/Getty Images Plus/GettyImages; p. 16 (yellow mug): serggn/iStock/Getty Images Plus/GettyImages; p. 16 (orange mug): Markus Guhl/Stockbyte/GettyImages; p. 16 (red mug): ampols/iStock/Getty Images Plus/GettyImages; p. 16 (pink mug): Pavlo Vakhrushev/Hemera/Getty Images Plus/GettyImages; p. 16 (purple mug): Ozii45/iStock/Getty Images Plus/GettyImages; p. 16 (brown mug): spaxiax/iStock/Getty Images Plus/GettyImages; p. 16 (black mug): DaddyBit/iStock/Getty Images Plus/GettyImages; p. 16 (gray mug): ambassador806/iStock/Getty Images Plus/GettyImages; p. 17 (B): londoneye/E+/GettyImages; p. 17: Nick David/Iconica/GettyImages; p. 17: londoneye/Vetta/GettyImages; p. 19 (tie): Phil Cardamone/E+/GettyImages; p. 19 (bracelet): Elnur Amikishiyev/Hemera/Getty Images Plus/GettyImages; p. 19 (ring): frender/iStock/Getty Images Plus/GettyImages; p. 19 (shirt): gofotograf/iStock/Getty Images Plus/GettyImages; p. 19 (belt): clark_fang/iStock/Getty Images Plus/GettyImages; p. 19 (earrings): Tarzhanova/iStock/Getty Images Plus/GettyImages; p. 19 (flip flops): subjug/E+/GettyImages; p. 19 (socks): Gary Ombler/Dorling Kindersley/GettyImages; p. 19 (B): Klaus Vedfelt/Iconica/GettyImages; p. 20 (jacket): White Packert/The Image Bank/GettyImages; p. 20 (coat): Steve Gorton/Dorling Kindersley/GettyImages; p. 20 (orange sweater): ARSELA/iStock/Getty Images Plus/GettyImages; p. 20 (grey sweater): popovaphoto/iStock/Getty Images Plus/GettyImages; p. 20 (gold rings): Tarek El Sombati/E+/GettyImages; p. 20 (silver rings): Burazin/Photographer's Choice/GettyImages; p. 21 (TR): Ivo Peer/EyeEm/GettyImages; p. 21 (TL): martinedoucet/E+/GettyImages; p. 21 (BR): Richard Boll/Photographer's Choice/GettyImages; p. 21 (BL): Al Freni/The LIFE Images Collection/GettyImages; p. 22 (header), p. vi (Unit 4): Westend61/GettyImages; p. 22 (T): Philip Othberg/EyeEm/GettyImages; p. 23 (T): Mark Metcalfe/Getty Images Entertainment/GettyImages; p. 23 (C): Leon Bennett/WireImage/GettyImages; p. 23 (Seth): Halfpoint/iStock/Getty Images Plus/GettyImages; p. 23 (Leanne): Caiaimage/Martin Barraud/Caiaimage/GettyImages; p. 23 (B): Ollie Millington/WireImage/GettyImages; p. 24 (Adele): Joern Pollex/Getty Images Entertainment/GettyImages; p. 24 (Steph Curry): TPG/Getty Images Entertainment/GettyImages; p. 24 (Star Wars): Bravo/NBCUniversal/GettyImages; p. 24 (Top chef): Atlaspix/Alamy; p. 25 (Alexis): Todor Tsvetkov/E+/GettyImages; p. 25 (Jacob): Neustockimages/E+/GettyImages; p. 25 (Tyler): fotostorm/E+/GettyImages; p. 25 (Andrew): panic_attack/iStock/Getty Images Plus/GettyImages; p. 25 (B): Henrik Sorensen/Iconica/GettyImages; p. 25 (Connor): Hero Images/GettyImages; p. 25 (Camila): Tetra Images/Brand X Pictures/GettyImages; p. 27 (B): STAN HONDA/AFP/GettyImages; p. 27 (C): Noel Vasquez/GC Images/GettyImages; p. 27 (T): Michael Tran/FilmMagic/GettyImages; p. 28 (leather jacket): deniztuyel/iStock/Getty Images Plus/GettyImages; p. 28 (wool jacket): Leonid Nyshko/iStock/Getty Images Plus/GettyImages; p. 28 (silk shirt): popovaphoto/iStock/Getty Images Plus/GettyImages; p. 28 (cotton shirt): gofotograf/iStock/Getty Images Plus/GettyImages; p. 28 (laptop): MyImages_Micha/iStock/Getty Images Plus/GettyImages; p. 28 (desktop computer): Ryan McVay/Photodisc/GettyImages; p. 29: Chad Slattery/The Image Bank/GettyImages; p. 30 (header), p. vi (Unit 5): eli_asenova/E+/GettyImages; p. 30 (James): alvarez/E+/GettyImages; p. 30 (Betty): Image Source/GettyImages; p. 30 (Robert): Siri Stafford/Stone/GettyImages; p. 30 (Patricia): Courtney Keating/E+/GettyImages; p. 30 (Deborah): Juanmonino/E+/GettyImages; p. 30 (Arturo): Kevin Dodge/Blend Images/GettyImages; p. 30 (Joseph): Izabela Habur/E+/GettyImages; p. 30 (Keiko): Paul Simcock/Blend Images/GettyImages; p. 30 (Joshua): Liam Norris/Cultura/GettyImages; p. 30 (Nicole): Westend61/Brand X Pictures/GettyImages; p. 30 (Veronica): lukas_zb/iStock/Getty Images Plus/GettyImages; p. 30 (Andrew): BDLM/Cultura/GettyImages; p. 30 (Emily): Robert Daly/Caiaimage/GettyImages; p. 30 (Alyssa): Westend61/GettyImages; p. 30 (Ethan): Compassionate Eye Foundation/Photodisc/GettyImages; p. 31 (Quincy Jones): Jason LaVeris/FilmMagic/GettyImages; p. 31 (Rashida Jones): Barry King/FilmMagic/GettyImages; p. 31 (Ashton Kutcher): JB Lacroix/WireImage/GettyImages; p. 31 (Mila Kunis): Vera Anderson/WireImage/GettyImages; p. 31 (Emma Roberts): Noam Galai/Getty Images North America/GettyImages; p. 31 (Julia Roberts): Dan MacMedan/WireImage/GettyImages; p. 31 (Cameron Diaz): Jason LaVeris/FilmMagic/GettyImages; p. 31 (Nicole Richie): Jeffrey Mayer/WireImage/GettyImages; p. 31 (BL): Vladimir Serov/Blend Images/GettyImages; p. 31 (Max): Flashpop/DigitalVision/GettyImages; p. 31 (Tina): Michael Blann/Iconica/GettyImages; p. 31 (BR): Oliver Strewe/Lonely Planet Images/GettyImages; p. 32 (man calling): Jed Share/Kaoru Share/Blend Images/GettyImages; p. 32 (woman calling): Justin Lambert/DigitalVision/GettyImages; p. 32 (woman chatting): Johnny Greig/iStock/Getty Images Plus/GettyImages; p. 32 (girl chatting): Tim Robberts/The Image Bank/GettyImages; p. 33 (T): Stuart Fox/Gallo Images/GettyImages; p. 33 (B): David Sacks/DigitalVision/GettyImages; p. 33 (C): Aping Vision/STS/Photodisc/GettyImages; p. 33 (Luis): yellowdog/Image Source/GettyImages; p. 33 (Vicky): XiXinXing/GettyImages; p. 34 (T): Robert Daly/Caiaimage/GettyImages; p. 34 (B): Nerida McMurray Photography/DigitalVision/GettyImages; p. 35 (TR): Hero Images/GettyImages; p. 35 (TL): Francesco Ridolfi/Cultura/GettyImages; p. 35 (BR): Compassionate Eye Foundation/Natasha Alipour Faridani/DigitalVision/GettyImages; p. 35 (BL): Edgardo Contreras/Taxi/GettyImages; p. 36 (header), p. vi (Unit 6): Thomas Barwick/DigitalVision/GettyImages; p. 36 (TL): Thomas Barwick/Stone/GettyImages; p. 36 (TR): RuslanDashinsky/iStock/Getty Images Plus/GettyImages; p. 36 (swimming fins): Bluemoon Stock/Stockbyte/GettyImages; p. 36 (shoes): yasinguneysu/E+/GettyImages; p. 36 (golf ball): Duncan Babbage/E+/GettyImages; p. 36 (volley ball): pioneer111/iStock/Getty Images Plus/GettyImages; p. 36 (karate uniform): Comstock/Stockbyte/GettyImages; p. 36 (fitness ball): ayzek/iStock/Getty Images Plus/GettyImages; p. 36 (yoga mat): Serg Myshkovsky/E+/GettyImages; p. 36 (soccer ball): Creative Crop/DigitalVision/GettyImages; p. 36 (bicycle): Comstock/Stockbyte/GettyImages; p. 37 (TR): Mike Kemp/Blend Images/GettyImages; p. 37 (TL): Tim Kitchen/The Image Bank/GettyImages; p. 39 (TR): Jon Bradley/The Image Bank/GettyImages; p. 39 (BR): Studio J Inc/GettyImages; p. 39 (Steph): ATELIER CREATION PHOTO/iStock/Getty Images Plus/GettyImages; p. 39 (Mick): ATELIER CREATION PHOTO/iStock/Getty Images Plus/GettyImages; p. 40 (T): ImagesBazaar/GettyImages; p. 40 (Ex 12.1): Ann Summa/Photolibrary/GettyImages; p. 40 (Ex 12.2): Portra Images/Iconica/GettyImages; p. 40 (Ex 12.3): mediaphotos/E+/GettyImages; p. 40 (Ex 12.4): T.T/Stone/GettyImages; p. 41 (T): Maximilian Stock Ltd./The Image Bank/GettyImages; p. 41 (BR): Gary Burchell/DigitalVision/GettyImages; p. 42: Hero Images/GettyImages; p. 43: Diana Mulvihill/The Image Bank/GettyImages; p. 44 (header), p. vi (Unit 7): edwardolive/iStock/Getty Images Plus/GettyImages; p. 44 (social media): sturti/iStock/Getty Images Plus/GettyImages; p. 44 (go dancing): Tom Merton/Caiaimage/GettyImages; p. 44 (listen to music): Sam Edwards/Caiaimage/GettyImages; p. 44 (play video games): Robert Deutschman/DigitalVision/GettyImages; p. 44 (read): John Lund/Marc Romanelli/Blend Images/GettyImages; p. 44 (relax): SolStock/E+/GettyImages; p. 44 (spend time): Image Source/GettyImages; p. 44 (watch TV): Dan Dalton/Caiaimage/GettyImages; p. 44 (CR): Caiaimage/Paul Bradbury/OJO+/GettyImages; p. 44 (BR): Hero Images/GettyImages; p. 44 (Cara): Caiaimage/Paul Bradbury/OJO+/GettyImages; p. 44 (Neil): Ezra Bailey/Taxi/GettyImages; p. 45: Westend61/GettyImages; p. 46: chinaface/E+/GettyImages; p. 47 (T): AleksandarNakic/E+/GettyImages; p. 47 (B): Songquan Deng/iStock/Getty Images Plus/GettyImages; p. 48: Elena Elisseeva/iStock/Getty Images Plus/GettyImages; p. 49 (T): AYOTOGRAPHY/iStock/Getty Images Plus/GettyImages; p. 49 (C): Gato Desaparecido/Alamy; p. 49 (B): simon's photo/Moment/GettyImages; p. 50 (header), p. vi (Unit 8): GARDEL Bertrand/hemis.fr/GettyImages; p. 50: Miles Ertman/All Canada Photos/GettyImages; p. 52: Chris Bennett/GettyImages; p. 53 (downtown): Anne Sophie Dhainaut/EyeEm/GettyImages; p. 53 (suburb): Bob O'Connor/Stone/GettyImages; p. 53 (shopping district): Busà Photography/Moment/GettyImages; p. 53 (college campus): Witold Skrypczak/Lonely Planet Images/GettyImages; p. 53 (business district): Julian Elliott Photography/Photolibrary/GettyImages; p. 53 (theatre district): Jerry Driendl/Stone/GettyImages; p. 53 (industrial district): ULTRA.F/Taxi Japan/GettyImages; p. 53 (small town): Barry Winiker/Photolibrary/GettyImages; p. 53 (BR): UpperCut Images/Stockbyte/GettyImages; p. 53 (Alana): UpperCut Images/Stockbyte/GettyImages; p. 53 (Barry): franckreporter/E+/GettyImages; p. 54: Guillermo Murcia/Moment/GettyImages; p. 55 (T): Noriko Hayashi/Bloomberg/GettyImages; p. 55 (C): Alessandra Santorelli/REX/Shutterstock; p. 55 (B): migstock/Alamy; p. 114 (TL): wdstock/iStock/Getty Images Plus/GettyImages; p. 114 (BL): wdstock/iStock/Getty Images Plus/GettyImages; p. 114 (R): Hero Images/GettyImages; p. 115 (CL): Rachel Watson/The Image Bank/GettyImages; p. 115 (CR): GMVozd/E+/GettyImages; p. 115 (BL): Zero Creatives/Cultura/GettyImages; p. 115 (BC): Rosiane Goncalves/EyeEm/GettyImages; p. 115 (BR): Stuart O'Sullivan/Stone/GettyImages; p. 116 (TL): loops7/E+/GettyImages; p. 116 (TR): Richard Boll/Photographer's Choice/GettyImages; p. 116 (CL): Thomas Northcut/Photodisc/GettyImages; p. 116 (CR): makkayak/E+/GettyImages; p. 117 (TL): Hemera Technologies/PhotoObjects.net/Getty Images Plus/GettyImages; p. 117 (TR): by_nicholas/iStock/Getty Images Plus/GettyImages; p. 117 (BL): imagenavi/GettyImages; p. 117 (BR): dandanian/E+/GettyImages; p. 118 (bike riding): Phillip Suddick/Taxi/GettyImages; p. 118 (street fair): Hill Street Studios/Blend Images/GettyImages; p. 118 (dancing): Morsa Images/Iconica/GettyImages; p. 118 (laundry): AndreyPopov/iStock/Getty Images Plus/GettyImages; p. 118 (clean house): Alin Dragulin/Vico Collective/GettyImages; p. 119 (learning language): Westend61/GettyImages; p. 119 (raising child): kupicoo/E+/GettyImages; p. 119 (renovating house): Tetra Images/GettyImages; p. 119 (working in country): A. Chederros/ONKYO/GettyImages; p. 119 (writing blog): Hero Images/GettyImages; p. 119 (driving car): Weekend Images Inc./